Gestures

Other books by Roger E. Axtell:

Do's & Taboos Around the World, 2nd Edition, Wiley

The Do's & Taboos of International Trade: A Small Business Primer, Wiley

Do's & Taboos of Hosting International Visitors, Wiley

Gestures
The Do's and Taboos of
Body Language Around the World

Roger E. Axtell

Illustrated by Mike Fornwald

John Wiley & Sons, Inc.
New York • Chichester • Brisbane • Toronto • Singapore

Copyright © 1991 by Roger E. Axtell

Published by John Wiley & Sons, Inc.

All rights reserved. Published simultaneously in Canada.

Library of Congress Cataloging-in-Publication Data

Axtell, Roger E.
     Gestures: the do's and taboos of body language around the world /
by Roger E. Axtell.
         p.   cm.
     Includes index.
     ISBN 0-471-53672-5
     1. Gesture—Cross-cultural studies.   2. Nonverbal communication
(Psychology)—Cross-cultural studies.   3. Nonverbal communication—
Cross-cultural studies.   I. Title.
     BF637.N66A88   1991
     153.6′9—dc20   91-8001

Printed in the United States of America

10 9 8 7 6 5

Printed and bound by the Courier Companies, Inc.

To Mardi, Kathi, and Roger . . .

No mere gesture here.
I want to record it clearly for you to know:
I am proud of each of you . . .
and love you even more.

Contents

Acknowledgments

Any book on gestures and cross-cultural communication owes an impossible indebtedness to one man, Desmond Morris, and to one unrelated institution, the David M. Kennedy Center for International Studies at Brigham Young University, Provo, Utah.

Desmond Morris is a British social anthropologist, a keen observer of the human condition, and a prolific writer on the subject of both human and animal behavior. In 1977, Morris produced a glorious book titled *Manwatching* (H. N. Abrams). He followed that in 1979 with *Gestures* (Stein and Day), which carefully catalogs 20 common gestures found in Europe. Anyone interested in a more scholarly treatment on all aspects of gestures and body language would be enriched by studying each of these.

At the David M. Kennedy Center for International Studies at Brigham Young University, *V. Lynn Tyler* has unselfishly helped me with each of my books. He is a kind, generous, and gracious man and the Kennedy Center contains a rich supply of material on cross-cultural behavior and communication. The Center offers a treasure of information to the public. One of the gems in their collection is called *CULTURGRAMS*, a series of four-page newsletters, one for each of about 100 different countries. *CULTURGRAMS* provides easily digestible information for each country on: customs and courtesies, the people, lifestyle, the nation, and references for additional study. Write to the Publication Services, David M. Kennedy Center for International Studies, 280 HRCB, Brigham Young University, Provo, Utah, 84602 for information on *CULTURGRAMS* and a complete listing of their many other publications.

Mike Fornwald's great talent is evident in the drawings throughout this book. His years of training and discipline in illustrating for animated films, plus his skill in political cartooning, enhanced his illustrations for this book. Moreover, he has been a delightful collaborator at every step while also serving as art director for a Chicago advertising agency.

A corps of others assisted me with information and by helping to check and recheck the hundreds of gestural entries throughout this book.

Susan Van Mell, a professional market researcher, contacted numerous embassies in the United States for affirmation, corrections and additions to our research. Her daughter, Trina, not only has an attentive and intelligent mother, but soon the marketing profession around Madison, WI, will also be graced with Susan's talents.

I met *Ingeborg Hegenbart* in Charlotte, NC, in 1987, and both my writing and speaking careers have benefited ever since. Ingeborg is president of Southern International Corp., a division of Southern National Bank, and as energetic and knowledgeable as one person can be in international business. She is also Dutch by birth, accent and inclination, and helped me check and verify every entry pertaining to The Netherlands.

For things Italian, I turned to the fabulous *Fantacci* family, friends and business associates for 35 years. The patriarch, Giuseppe, must have provided the model for the wonderfully warm "Most Unforgettable Characters" series in the READER'S DIGEST magazine of many years ago. "Beppe" has been an inspiration to me, and his son, Bert, a great and much admired friend.

For material on Latin America, I received great assistance from *Jack* and *Marie Ottiker,* lifelong residents of that area. Marie is an accomplished writer and Jack is a former executive with several major U.S. corporations. He is more recently president of the American Chamber of Commerce in Lima, Peru.

Professor Robert T. Moran is, in my view, the pre-eminent educator in cross-cultural behavior, especially for business. Bob is professor of International Studies and Director of the Program in Cross-Cultural Communication at "Thunderbird," officially known as the American Graduate School of International Management, Glendale, AZ. He and Philip R. Harris co-authored the textbook *Managing Cultural Differences* (Gulf Publishing Co., 3rd Ed., 1991).

Barbara Moebius is Program Director of the International Trade Program at the Waukesha County Technical College, Pewaukee, WI. Barb has not only developed probably the best repository of international business research material in the Mid-West, but has also directed a burgeoning program of training young people for lifetime careers in international business.

Eugene Theroux is an internationally known legal expert, especially on The People's Republic of China and the U.S.S.R. Gene is also an equally talented writer and artist. He, along with Fredric M. Kaplan, wrote *The HarperCollins Business Guide to Moscow* (Harper & Row, 1990) an indispensable guide to anyone traveling to that city.

For gestures in Scandinavia, to review my research I turned to a 30-year friend and business associate named *Klavs Olsen* of Copenhagen. Klavs not only has extensive business interests in Norway, Sweden and Finland but serves as President of the Danish Association of Business (comparable to a Chamber of Commerce in the United States).

To all of the above, I offer a deep Japanese bow, an Irish tip of the hat, a hearty Chinese toast, and a good old-fashioned American salute . . . gestures all, in gratitude and thanks.

Last, my most valuable resource, asset, partner, and best earthly friend (also, my collaborator in producing three wonderful children) has been, and is, my wife, Mitzi. I owe her more—much more—than mere acknowledgments.

ROGER E. AXTELL

Janesville, Wisconsin

Introduction

Over the past decade, I have presented hundreds of speeches, seminars, and workshops on the often amusing subject of international behavior. I found myself automatically saving the segment on gestures for the end of each presentation because audiences seemed to enjoy it so much. After these programs, people invariably came to me to relate their own amusing, provocative, and sometimes distressing experiences with gestures and body language around the globe.

No market research could so clearly substantiate interest in this subject. This book, then, results from an accumulation of more than 10 years of research, including recent research visits to England, West Germany, France, Yugoslavia, Greece, Italy, Hong Kong, Thailand, Malaysia, Indonesia, and the Philippines. It also benefits from the labor of Susan Van Mell, a professional research specialist who helped me recheck, verify, and amplify some of the material.

All this reinforced a conviction that gestures are powerful communicators used by a wide and growing number of internationally cosmopolitan individuals. One has only to view a current news show on television to see the importance of gestures in our culture as Saudis, Russians, Chinese, and numerous others speak into the ubiquitous camera.

How This Book Is Organized

This book is divided into six chapters. The premise of Chapter 1, illustrated with numerous examples, is that gestures and body language are not only powerful communicators but that different cultures use gestures and body language in dramatically different ways.

Chapter 2 discusses the most popular gestures found around the world, beginning with how we *greet* one another. Shaking hands is by no means a universal greeting; in fact, there are at least a half-dozen other social greetings—even several different ways of shaking hands.

1

We next deal with "beckoning" gestures. Different cultures have different ways to relay the message "Hey! Come here." For example, on one occasion in Buenos Aires, when my host dropped me off at the hotel entrance, I waved goodbye as he drove away. To my amazement he stopped the car, got out, and came back and asked what I wanted. With that incident, I learned that waving goodbye American-style could in Argentina actually mean "Hey! Come back." (See page 28 for a more complete explanation.)

The next discussion focuses on "insulting" gestures from around the world. We include this discussion not to increase your repertoire, but to help you avoid embarrassment. Gestures you probably employ safely and routinely each day are considered not only rude but obscene in certain other parts of the world.

Following that, you will find a useful exposition on *touching*. While some cultures eschew bodily contact in almost all business and social situations, others actually expect it.

Chapter 2 also takes four common gestures and illustrates the *ying* and *yang* (or opposite) meanings of each, depending on where you are in the world. Those four common gestures are: (1) The "O.K." signal—thumb and forefinger forming a circle, with the other three fingers splayed outward; (2) the "thumbs up" gesture; (3) the "V for victory" signal—index and middle finger forming a V; and (4) the "vertical horns," or what we have chosen to call the "hook 'em horns" gesture—a fist with the index and little fingers extended. Each of these four gestures is illustrated and examined anecdotally. My hope is that through stories and drawings, you can see how seemingly common gestures like these can get you into a world of trouble.

Chapter 3 is designed to help you learn or trace a particular gesture, using scores of drawings from the talented hand and art board of illustrator Mike Fornwald. To help you track down a specific gesture or action, Chapter 3 is organized from head to toe, literally. Therefore, if you want to know about a particular gesture you observed involving, say, the chin, you can readily find it between mouth and arms.

Chapter 4 describes what I have chosen to call the "Ultimate Gesture."

Chapter 5 provides a short list of important gestures to bear in mind.

In Chapter 6, you will find a country-by-country listing of common gestures and body language. The countries are grouped by major geographic region, starting with Europe, then the Middle East and Africa, followed by the Pacific and Asia, Central and South America, and finally the United States and Canada. This listing not only catalogs the commonly used gestures in each but cross-references them back to Chapter 3. Therefore, if you read a word description of a gesture in the country-by-country section and are unclear about what it looks like, you can examine an illustration of it in Chapter 3.

Now, an important disclaimer.

Any book on understanding human behavior is tricky stuff. No two people behave in precisely the same way. Nor do people from the same culture all perform exactly the same gestures and body language uniformly. For almost any gesture in this book there will probably be a minority within a given nationality who might say "Well, some might attach that meaning to it, but to me it means . . ." and then they will provide a different interpretation.

So, even among a single nationality, when dealing with hand and body signals, you will probably encounter that type of contradiction and clutter.

The clutter aside, the chief objective of this book is to help you learn *right* from *rude,* to help avoid misunderstandings.

The hope is that this book will enable you to become more sensitive, more aware, and more observant when it comes to effective, silent communications.

What is the value of avoiding just one misunderstanding? As a wise counselor once told me: "That's like trying to determine the value of a single light bulb. Unlit, the bulb has little value. Lit, the bulb can illuminate one room. And, one illuminated room occupied by one creative person can change the world."

1

The Power of Gestures

L ook around you.

The world is a giddy montage of vivid gestures—traffic police, street vendors, expressway drivers, teachers, children on playgrounds, athletes with their exuberant hugging, clenched fists and "high fives." People all over the world use their hands, heads, and bodies to communicate expressively.

Without gestures, our world would be static, colorless. The social anthropologist Edward T. Hall claims 60 percent of *all* our communication is nonverbal. In that case, how can we possibly communicate with one another without gestures?

We use gestures daily, almost instinctively, from beckoning to a waiter, or punctuating a business presentation with visual signals to airport ground attendants guiding an airline pilot into the jetway or a parent using a whole dictionary of gestures to teach (or preach to) a child.

Gestures can be menacing (two drivers on a freeway), warm (an open-armed welcome), instructive (a policeman giving road directions), or even sensuous (the languid movements of a Hawaiian hula dancer).

The premise of this book is not only that gestures are woven inextricably into our social lives, but also that the "vocabulary" of gestures, can be at once informative and entertaining . . . but also dangerous. For while great enjoyment can come from learning the odd, sometimes contradictory meanings of gestures we tend to take for granted, some innocent-appearing gestures can generate genuine grief.

Example

An American teenager was hitch-hiking in Nigeria. A carload of locals passed him. The car screeched to a halt. The locals jumped out and promptly roughed up the visitor. Why? Because in Nigeria, the gesture commonly used in America for hitch-hiking (thumb extended upward) is considered a very rude signal.

Conversely, gestures can be fun, impulsive, and irresistible:

Example

In 1990, *National Geographic Magazine* lined up all the members of the U.S. Supreme Court for an official photograph. Justice Sandra Day O'Connor found herself standing behind Justice Byron White. According to news reports, Justice O'Connor apparently could not resist the impulse shared by children and adults for decades—she quietly formed a "V" with her fingers and held them just above

White's head, forming the old "rabbit ears" sign. Even the loftiest jurists in the land cannot resist the urge to flash an impish gesture from time to time.

Gestures and body language communicate as effectively as words—maybe even more effectively. Take a baby's smile. Can words possibly duplicate that wonderfully unique sight? It is not by accident, it seems, that as infants we learn the signal of smiling before we learn to talk. Also, according to a 1991 report in *Science* magazine, deaf babies "babble" with their hands in the same way hearing babies string sounds together before they learn to speak. Deaf babies form repetitive signals with their hands before they are 10 months old, paralleling hearing infants who begin trying out sounds that evolve into spoken language.

Some anthropologists divide our actions and gestures into three broad categories: instinctive, coded and acquired. When a baby laughs in response to stimuli or sucks on a nipple, such actions are clearly instinctive. Coded or technical gestures operate via pre-established agreement, such as those used by firemen, TV directors or mariners. (Sign language, including the manual alphabet, is a rich and varied example of coded gestures.)

This book, however, will concentrate on *acquired* gestures— those used around the world to accompany day-to-day communication. The emphasis will be on how identical acquired gestures mean different things among different countries. Since we use these acquired gestures unconsciously, it behooves us to become more conscious of what we are signaling and how those signals may be misinterpreted. Each society has its own rules for gestures. Here's just one example:

Example

Nowhere in the United States, or in many other countries for that matter, can a person in any public situation casually pat or pinch another person on their derriere. In Rome, on the famous Via Veneto, a pinch may be accepted with impunity, but it's absolutely forbidden in other places around the world. In fact, in many places one might even get arrested for trying it.

But there is one exception—an aberration that occurs among football players in America (and soccer players in Europe). Surely you've noticed; from defensive back to tight-end, these bruisers seem to have a fetish for fanny-patting. To compliment a teammate or exhort them to play harder, hulking linemen on American professional football teams slap the rumps of other team members. And it is perfectly acceptable behavior. But—and this is important—while they can pat and slap, *they must never linger!* That would send quite a different signal, indeed.

THE SCIENCE OF GESTURES

Next time you step on to an *elevator,* try this experiment. It demonstrates how, even in the most mundane situations, we have a silent set of rules for bodily behavior in public settings.

Here is the setting:

If there are only one or two people on an elevator, they usually lean against the walls of the elevator. If four people board the elevator, the four corners are usually occupied.

However, when the population reaches five or six people, everyone begins to obey more complex rules of elevator etiquette. It is almost like a ritualistic dance. They all turn to face the door. "They get taller and thinner," as psychologist Layne Longfellow describes it. "Hands and purses and briefcases hang down in front of the body—that's called The Fig Leaf Position, by the way. They mustn't touch each other in any way unless the elevator is crowded, and then only at the shoulder or lightly against the upper arm. Also, there is a tendency to look upward at the illuminated floor indicator. If they speak, it is definitely *sotto voce.*"

If you doubt this is standard—almost sacred—elevator behavior, then try this: Next time you walk on to a crowded elevator, *don't turn around and face the door.* Instead, just stand there facing the others. If you want to create even more tension, grin. Very likely the other passengers will glare back, surprised, grim, and upset. Reason? You have broken the rules.

One person who tried this experiment actually heard someone in the back of the elevator whisper "Call 911. We've got a real weirdo here."

The technical term for such behavior is "elevator proxemics," meaning how people space themselves on elevators. In fact, *proxemics* is an acknowledged area of study within psychology. There are kindred branches as well. For example, *kinesics* is the study of body motion. Kinesicists analyze body movements in slow motion. Anthropologists have studied the kinesics of different cultures and substantiated that an Arab, an Englishman, and a Latino signal to each other in notably different ways.

A pioneer researcher in kinesics is Ray Birdwhistell, but there are many other respected authorities. The British social anthropologist Desmond Morris gained considerable celebrity in 1967 with his book *The Naked Ape* (Jonathan Cape, London). In 1977, he produced the wonderfully illustrated and written hallmark book in this field, entitled *Manwatching* (Abrams, New York). We owe a great deal to Morris for his keen observations and dedicated research.

Another communications expert, Mario Pei, once estimated that humans can produce up to 700,000 different physical signs. Birdwhistell estimates that the face alone is capable of producing 250,000 expressions and reports that researcher M. H. Krout identified 5,000 distinct hand gestures that he believed had verbal equivalents while another researcher in kinesics, G. W. Hewes, has cataloged 1,000 different postures and their accompanying gestures.

How does verbal communication compare to nonverbal communication? Author George du Maurier once commented that "[The spoken] Language is a poor thing. You fill your lungs with wind and shake a little slit in your throat, and make mouths, and that shakes the air; and the air shakes a pair of little drums in my head . . . and my brain seizes your meaning in the rough. What a roundabout way and what a waste of time."

Social scientist and author Flora Davis claims that gestures are shortcuts. They are much stronger than punctuation or the underscoring of words in bold-face type or italics, she says. "They are like the maestro's baton to each musician in the ensemble."

Finally, *Time* magazine, in an essay written by Frank Trippett and titled "Why So Much Is Beyond Words," contends that "Homo sapiens, as a communicator, does not seem to have come all that far from the time when grunts and gesticulations were the main ways of getting messages across. Both individuals and groups still send vital messages by gesture, by pantomime, by dramatics—by a dizzy diversity of what scholars call nonverbal communications."

While any book on gestures and body signals would naturally draw from the science of kinesics, or nonverbal communications, this is not a scientific text. Instead, it deals only with the first thin layer of that science: the collection of gestures and body language floating on the surface of a culture. But it is precisely that assortment of signals a world wanderer first encounters as a tourist, student, or businessperson.

GESTURES ARE IMPORTANT

Gestures and body language have been called "the silent language." The collection of true stories that follows demonstrates how that "silence" has its own special volume—and its own direct impact on our lives.

- In 1988 in Los Angeles, an entertainer from Thailand was convicted of the second-degree murder of a 29-year-old Laotian. The entertainer was singing in an after-hours Thai cabaret when the Laotion, a patron, put his foot on a chair with the sole directed at the singer. When the cabaret closed, the entertainer followed the man and shot him. Why? Among Southeast Asians, showing or directing the sole of the shoe to another person is considered a grievous insult.

- In Nairobi, Kenya, in 1990, a ruling party boss urged his followers to chop off the fingers of people who flashed a two-fingered salute in support of permitting opposition parties. The leader told members of his party's youth wing this would discourage others from flashing the opposition's salute.

From acts of violence like the two examples just mentioned, to the opposite end of the emotional spectrum—signs of love— our body actions are powerful signs. David Givens, author of *Love Signals* (Crown, New York, 1983) claims that men and women unconsciously shrug their shoulders when they find each other attractive. Also, a woman attracted to a man will tilt her head down and to the side, then look in his direction in a coy or coquettish way. Let's look at some other examples.

- An American woman gets into a car with an American man, slides over to his side, and kisses him on the cheek. A common enough occurrence that probably happens hundreds of thousands of times each day in the United States. But in this case it happened in Saudi Arabia, where public displays of affection are disliked, even forbidden, and marriage is sacrosanct. The incident is reported by author Margaret K. Nydell, in her fascinating book *Understanding Arabs* (Intercultural Press, 1987). Nydell writes that the meeting between the man and woman happened to be seen by a captain of the Saudi National Guard who then demanded proof that the two were married. They were, but not to each other. "The woman was sent out of the country and the man, who compounded his problem by being argumentative, was sent to jail," Nydell writes.

- Just as love and affection can be signaled through actions and gestures, so can courage. A 12-year-old American boy known as "David" was born without an immune system to shield him against disease. He lived his entire life inside a sterile plastic bubble and thus became known as "the bubble boy." It was not until the final 15 days of his life when death was imminent that he emerged and, for the first time, experienced the touch of a hand unprotected by a glove, his mother's kiss, and the sensation of his mother running a comb through his long hair. As he lay dying he was conscious to the last. He made jokes and his final gesture, before he slipped into a sedated sleep that ended in death, was a wink at his doctor.

- Even the Queen of England has adopted special nonverbal signals. For example, you will probably never see her seated with her legs crossed *at the knees.* This is likely a vestige of Victorian days when "ladies" did not assume such a revealing posture. Instead, for English royalty, crossing the legs *at the ankles* is both proper and preferred.

- Queen Elizabeth II has also gone so far as to adopt certain body motions to signal messages to her entourage. Raymond Fullager, who writes and lectures about the royal family, claims Her Majesty uses *her purse* to send some 20 different signals to her staff. For example, when she shifts her handbag from her right arm to her left, it is a signal to her bodyguards to "Come and rescue me from this situation!"

- Winston Churchill is probably credited with putting the "V for victory" sign in both our history books and our contemporary usage. During World War II, the picture of Churchill flashing the famous "V" became a familiar sight. In fact, it became a rallying point for the Allied forces against the Axis armies. So powerful was this gesture that even today statues can be seen of Churchill and his "V" frozen in time. (For a full account on the use of the "V for victory" gesture, see page 51.)

- When American military forces were mobilized for the "Desert Shield" operation in Saudi Arabia in the late summer of 1990, along with weapons, ammunition, and desert gear they packed along a 40-page booklet on gestures and body language among the Arabs. For example, GIs were cautioned to refrain from gawking at Arab women, and not to even consider trying to date them. Other tips: Avoid crossing the legs so the sole of the shoe is pointed at someone; don't be upset if Arabs stand very close, even touch you, when conversing; don't admire an Arab's possessions because he may then feel required to give you the object of your admiration as a gift on the spot. He also will expect a gift in return. Finally, that the "O.K." gesture (thumb and forefinger forming a circle) may be interpreted there as giving a curse.

- Knowing body language can avoid potential diplomatic catastrophes at top government levels as well. Milton Neshek is an American lawyer and officer of a Japanese-owned company located in the North American Midwest. He once accompanied the governor of his state on a trade mission to Japan where the governor addressed a large and distinguished audience of Japanese officials. At the conclusion of the presentation, the visibly upset governor cornered Neshek and lamented "My speech was a disaster! I shouldn't have delivered it. Why didn't my staff warn me?" Confused, Neshek asked "What made you think it was so bad?" The governor complained he had seen many members of the audience asleep, even nodding their heads. Relieved, Neshek quickly explained that among the Japanese a common way to show concentration and attentiveness was to close the eyes in contemplation and nod the head slightly, up and down. What the governor read as boredom was actually a signal of respect and attention.

- The U.S. State Department recognizes the importance of bodily actions among other cultures. When I made my first business trip to The People's Republic of China in April, 1976, our group was given a special briefing in Washington, DC, because we were among the first businesspeople to travel to China after the détente arranged by President Nixon and Chairman Mao. Here are two relevant points extracted from that briefing:

  —Chinese generally do not touch a drink at the dinner table without proposing a toast to others at the table, even if only by raising the glass and making eye contact. Only a symbolic sip need be taken in reply. It is perfectly acceptable to explain that one does not drink at all, providing one is consistent.

  —Chinese are very sensitive to problems of precedence at doorways, in automobiles, and so on. Even a token gesture of yielding the right of way or the seat of honor to a Chinese is appreciated; failure to make the gesture when expected could be interpreted as arrogance.

- Eugene Theroux is a widely traveled international legal expert, having managed his law firm's offices in both the People's Republic of China and in the U.S.S.R. "I was once startled," he writes, "in a negotiation in China to notice that the chief negotiator on the other side suddenly bent forward and began to press

13

his temples with the two first fingers of each hand. I thought perhaps my negotiating style had driven him to the breaking point, until he smiled and explained that this is an acupressure technique for reducing stress." Theroux added, "And by the way, it works!"

• In commercial transactions, some Chinese buyers and sellers may be seen using an ancient, esoteric method of hand gestures to conduct business in secret. It is a secret bidding code. A buyer and seller will each place one hand under a cloth or some other cover. Then the bidder says only "hundred" or "thousand" out loud. Meanwhile, under the cloth, the bidder extends certain fingers of the hidden hand to indicate how many units he is bidding. If he says "thousand," and extends two fingers, that means 2,000; if he extends four fingers, it means 4,000, and so on.

• Author Helen Colton, in her book *The Gift of Touch* (Seaview/Putnam, 1983), graphically describes how different cultures react with varying gestures. In this case, she poses an embarrassing situation and tells how various people around the world would react. The situation: You suddenly come upon a strange woman in her bath. The varied reactions of that woman would be as follows:

—A Mohammedan woman would cover her face.

—A Laotian woman would cover her breasts.

—A Chinese woman (before the Revolution) would hide her feet.

—In Sumatra, the woman would conceal her knees.

—In Samoa, she would cover her navel.

—In the Western world, she would cover her breasts with one arm and her genital area with the other hand.*

• In 1968, the international sports world was shocked by a single arm and hand gesture. The scene appeared in photographs on newspaper front pages all over the world. At the 1968 Olympic games in Mexico City, two black Americans were strongly favored to win medals in the 200-meter race. Tommie Smith and John Carlos were students at San Jose State College and members of a group of athletes organized to protest the treatment of

* Excerpts reprinted by permission of the Putnam Publishing Group from THE GIFT OF TOUCH by Helen Colton. Copyright © 1983 by Helen Colton.

blacks in the United States. Smith won the gold and Carlos the bronze medal. At the medal awards ceremony, when the U.S. national anthem was played, spectators were stunned to see Smith and Carlos ascend the platform in bare feet, bow their heads, and raise one black-gloved hand in the black-power salute. They later explained that their clenched fists symbolized black strength and unity and their bare feet signaled a reminder of black poverty in the United States. Their bowed heads, they said, signaled their belief that the words of freedom in the U.S. national anthem applied only to Americans with white skin. Their actions created a sensation and the U.S. Olympic Committee suspended the two athletes and commanded them to leave the Olympic village.

- Virtually everywhere in the world clapping one's hands together in applause is a signal of honor, adulation, enjoyment, or approval. (Incidentally, you can detect whether a person is right-handed or left-handed by observing by the way they applaud. A right-handed person will slap that hand down into and on top of the left palm; a left-handed person will make the left hand dominant.) In the United States, clapping at large public events is often accompanied by whistling; however, in much of Europe, such whistling is a signal of derision and disapproval. In China, the customary way to greet visitors is with applause.

- How do the *deaf* signal applause? After all, they cannot hear the gratifying sound produced by applause. The answer is that they have adopted their own unique method of signaling enjoyment or approval. They raise their hands to shoulder or head height, palms outward, and shake them with a fast, almost shivering-like motion. Seeing an audience waggling their hands in that fashion can be just as rewarding as hearing a thundering round of applause.

- One would naturally believe that conducting a philharmonic orchestra relied solely on one sense: Hearing. But the conductor of the Buffalo, New York, Philharmonic Orchestra, interviewed on National Public Radio, explained that "Conducting is, in fact, a visual art. Through small gestures one influences the whole performance and its outcome."

- Some examples of gestures can seem almost amazing, even miraculous. Moments after being blessed by John Paul II at the Vatican, Jan Lavric, a visiting doctor from London, stunned bystanders by abruptly standing up, getting out of his wheelchair and walking away. What appeared as a miracle was explained later by Lavric: "I was tired and sat down in an empty wheelchair.

15

Suddenly, a nun wheeled me off, and before I could explain, the Pope blessed me."

• Gestures can also be a valuable form of opinion polling. According to *People* magazine, at least one U.S. politician had his own system of gauging his popularity. "I watch the crowds waving to me," he explained, "and I count the number of fingers they're using."

CONCLUSION

This book is intended to put you *en garde* —appropriately, a classic protective stance from the sport of fencing. As the global village continues to shrink and cultures collide, it is more and more essential for all of us to become *en garde*, figuratively speaking, to the myriad motions, gestures, and body language that surround us each day.

Another apt French phrase is *beau geste*. It means, literally, a "beautiful gesture." It also served as the title of a well-remembered movie of the 1930s that related a heroic act of courage. It is an appropriate phrase for this book, and one worth remembering. As more of us cross over cultural borders, it would be our *beau geste* to learn, understand, and respect more about the silent but powerful language of gestures and body language.

The chapters that follow will help us do exactly that.

2

The Most Popular Gestures

If there are, indeed more than 700,000 different gestures that can be both powerful and contradictory, which gestures do we use the most?

In the 1970s, Desmond Morris (see Chapter 1) surveyed 1,200 informants in Western and Southern Europe plus some Mediterranean areas and developed a list of what he called the 20 key gestures.

If I were to list some of those 20—like "the fingers cross," "the eyelid pull," "the hand purse," and "the ear touch"—I doubt you would recognize them from those labels, much less categorize them as "most popular." By the time you finish this book, however, you will be able to recognize at least these 20 and understand their significance in a wide variety of cultures.

This chapter concentrates on four *general categories* of gestures:

- Greetings gestures

- Beckoning gestures

- Insulting gestures

- Touching gestures

and four *specific,* common and popular gestures:

- "O.K." signal

- "Thumbs up"

- "V for victory"

- Vertical horns (or "hook 'em horns")

As you will see, just these eight types of popular gestures provide a dizzying variety of usages and meanings.

Among those eight groups of signals, you will quickly recognize a gesture and know its meaning . . . that is, the meaning according to *your* society, *your* geography, and *your* ethnic influences. The *other* interpretations from around the world for that same gesture should prove both informative and entertaining. In fact, knowledge of these varied interpretations might some day save you from a stern look, a strained relationship, or possibly even a smashed nose.

Example

An engineer for a New Jersey plastics machinery company relates this story: His firm purchased a German company in the same field and the two firms began exchanging engineers for purposes of product familiarization. One day, an American and German engineer were working side-by-side on a new machine. "Try increasing the pressure," the American suggested. The German did so, saying "How is that? Did I do that correctly?" The American replied by gesturing, making a circle with his thumb and forefinger, a sign used throughout North America to mean "O.K." The German abruptly put down his tools and walked away. He refused any further communication with the American. Finally, a supervisor forced the two men to sit down and reconstruct what happened. It seems that, to a German, when someone forms a thumb and forefinger in a circle, as the American had done, it signifies "You asshole."

To begin our study of popular gestures and how they can be misinterpreted depending on the country, we begin with the way most relationships begin: With the first handshake.

GREETINGS

"When you shake hands," my father used to growl at me, "be sure you give 'em a good, firm grip. Also, look 'em straight in the eye."
    Little did I realize that in other parts of the world fathers were teaching their sons and daughters something entirely different.
    For example, fathers in India were instructing their children the *namaste* (Figure 2.1), where the hands are placed in a praying position, about chest high, accompanied by a slight bow. It also means "thank you" and "I'm sorry." In Thailand, this same gentle

Figure 2.1   A man from India greeting a Westerner with a *namaste*.

and gracious gesture is called the *wai*. Don't get carried away and lift the pressed hands above the head, however, or it could be construed as an insult.

The exact origins of both the handshake and *namaste* are unclear. Citizens of the Roman empire greeted each other with a hand-and-forearm clasp, but some anthropologists believe our handshake of today may be only a couple hundred years old.

Whatever the genesis, the intent seems clear. Whether it's the outstretched hand, or the palms pressed together, each signal suggests openness and a clear sign that the greeter is not carrying a weapon.

Some believe the hug or embrace originally had a similar purpose: The assurance that no weapons were hidden beneath the flowing robes worn from the time of the Egyptians through the Middle Ages.

Another sign of openness when we greet one another involves the eyes and forehead. Anthropologists point out that when humans greet, regardless of our nationality or race, we all open our eyes wider than normal and our foreheads wrinkle. Since the eyebrows move upward, this is often referred to as the "eyebrow flash." Both motions appear to be instinctive and signal openness and are, therefore, a form of greeting.

There are other more exotic forms of greetings as well. In the Middle East, the older generation can still be seen giving the *salaam*. In this signal, the right hand sweeps upward, first touching the heart, then the forehead and finally up and outward, perhaps with a slight nod of the head (Figure 2.2). The words that accompany this greeting are, *salaam alaykum* meaning, appropriately, "Peace be with you."

Figure 2.2   The *salaam*, a Middle-Eastern greeting.

Another version of the *salaam* is found in Malaysia: One stretches out the hands, touches fingertips, and then returns the hands to the chest. (Not done, however, between members of the opposite sex.)

The Hollywood movie industry popularized the stereotype of a tall, bronze-skinned American Indian standing with palm upraised, saying "How." As every American school child knows, that was the way all Indians greeted the pale-faced settlers. At least that is what Hollywood would have us believe. True or not, it is a fact that communication between different tribes of native Americans and the first white explorers was solely through sign language. Therefore, the simple, raised palm as a form of greeting was critical to the exploration and opening of the U.S. West.

Greetings can also convey secret messages. On my last trip to the Mediterranean area, I was told that in many countries there, a greeting among homosexual men is to shake hands in a very specific and hidden manner: with the middle finger folded down into the palm.

Greetings can be downright physical, too, to the point you may want to wear a football helmet and shoulder pads. Eskimos greet each other by banging the other party with a hand either on the head or shoulders. Polynesian men who are strangers welcome each other by embracing and then rubbing each other's back. Among the Matavai, friends who have been parted for some time scratch each other's head and temples with the tip of a shark's tooth, often drawing blood.

The Maori tribespeople in New Zealand choose even today to greet each other with a gesture that seems to epitomize closeness and friendship: They rub noses (Figure 2.3). The Eskimos use this same gesture, but with more personal meaning.

Some East African tribes greet each other by spitting at each other's feet. And for perhaps the most unusual and mysterious greeting, Tibetan tribesmen are said to greet each other quite warmly by *sticking out their tongues* at each other.

Let's return to the more familiar gesture of greeting, the handshake. While *my* father was drilling me with "Firm handshake, direct eye contact," fathers in the Middle East were instructing their sons "When you shake hands, a *gentle* grip is appropriate. Don't grip the hand firmly. A firm grip suggests aggression. And in places like Japan and Korea, fathers were not only advocating "Yes, gentle, not firm" but were adding "and try to avoid direct eye contact. Staring at someone is intimidating and disrespectful."

Among North Americans and many Europeans, gripping a limp hand is distasteful. They liken it to being weak and effeminate. A simile often used is that it is like "grasping a dead fish."

Figure 2.3   The Maori Greeting.

Some people believe Americans go too far in the other direction, however. Prince Charles of England, who must be a connoisseur on greetings by now, has complained of the finger-crunching grip of the Americans. "Especially Texans," he adds.

Handshakes can be either "gentle," "firm," or "Texan." But there is more than just hand pressure involved in the business of shaking hands.

In Northern Europe, you are most likely to receive a curt, firm, one-pump handshake. Also, women and children there will customarily extend their hand in greeting, whereas in the parts of North America and in the Far East, women will only occasionally take that initiative. The same is true for children.

In Islamic countries, it is forbidden for unrelated men to touch women, so men should never offer to shake hands with women there. West African male friends will often add a snappy finish to a handshake as follows: as they release the grip, each middle finger is pressed together and then snapped abruptly into the fleshy pad below the thumb.

The French seem to be the most "handshakingest" of all. Visitors remark on how the French seem to shake hands when greeting, when departing, when returning . . . and repeat the custom each morning of every day, no matter if the relationship is business or social. Author Peter Mayle, in his engaging book *A Year in Provence* (Knopf, 1990), explains that if a Frenchman happens to have soiled hands he will offer his forearm in greeting, or if he is holding packages he will even extend a little finger to be grasped.

In South America, Bolivians win the title of "Greatest Greeters." Whenever two friends meet and chat, their greeting usually includes a handshake and a hearty clap on the back.

Psychologists regard the handshake as one of the most powerful of all tactile contacts, so maybe there's something to be learned from the French and the Bolivians.

In Southern Europe and Central and South America, the handshake will usually be warmer and probably a bit longer, frequently accompanied by the left hand touching the other person's forearm, elbow, or even lapel.

A version popular in American politics is to shake hands using the free hand to cover the grip. On the scale of warmth of a greeting, this gesture supposedly adds several degrees of closeness and implied unity.

In the Soviet Union, good male friends will start with a strong, firm handshake and then continue forward into the so-called "bear hug" so often identified with that country. But, just to demonstrate that common customs do not necessarily cross common boundaries, neighboring Finns firmly reject bear hugging. "Don't do it here," they warn. "We don't hug or kiss or have bodily contact with strangers like the Russians do."

In Latin American countries, the hug is called the *abrazo*, which means "embrace." It is often accompanied by a couple of hearty claps on the back (Figure 2.4). Most North Americans, Northern Europeans, and Orientals find any such touching or hugging very uncomfortable.

My first encounter with the Latin *abrazo* occurred in the airport at Buenos Aires, Argentina, when I was very new to this game of gestures and greetings. There to meet me, arms outstretched, was the manager of our local company. "My God," I thought, "that man is going to hug me!" My life seemed to pass before my eyes. Walking forward stiffly, I forgot that one must move the head either right or left. We ended up smashing noses.

Now let us turn to that most courtly of all greetings, the *bow*. Veteran travelers to Japan counsel "When you visit Japan, keep

Figure 2.4 *Un abrazo* (embrace).

your shoes shined at all times, since everyone will be looking at them a lot when bowing." I am often asked "Should a North American or European bow to a Japanese?" No, it is not absolutely necessary, but a slight bow demonstrates that you respect their customs. And in Japan, where style and grace and courteousness are revered, that simple act would surely be noted, appreciated, and probably remembered. Think about the subtle psychology of this and all gestures. Do we expect other cultures to adopt our customs or are we willing to adopt theirs. This might translate to how business or even foreign relations are to be conducted. Do we compromise or force our associate to deal only on our terms. You may not have time to learn a language, but taking time to learn the "signals" is a powerful communicator.

Western business people stationed in Japan know this and take pains to carefully emulate the Japanese. But they also joke among themselves: "You know you've stayed in Japan too long when you have a telephone conversation and find yourself bowing into the telephone." (See Figure 2.5.)

Many Westerners view the bow as an act of subservience, but in Japan that would be completely wrong. For the Japanese a bow signals respect and humility, two qualities coveted throughout the Orient.

Westerners face many handicaps in trying to learn the complete art of Japanese bowing because there is so much hidden meaning in every dip and bob. For example:

• *Who bows first?*

• *How low does one bow?*

Figure 2.5

25

- *When do we shake hands?*
- *When do we exchange business cards?*

The answers are as follows:

Who bows first? And how low?
The operative word is *rank*. The shortcut for this lesson is simply to remember "The higher the rank of the person facing you, the lower you bow." In Japanese society, it is extremely important, especially in business, to know the rank of people with whom you come in contact. The same applies to the rank of your company. For example, the middle-level manager in a large powerful company outranks a department head from a smaller, less important company.

Therefore, who bows first and lowest? Answer: The person of lower rank bows first and lowest.

When do we shake hands?
The answer is complicated by the fact that many Japanese, especially those who travel abroad on business, are quickly adopting Western ways. As a result, our respective learning curves may collide midway. We may bow in respect to their practices, while they may simultaneously stick out their hand. They may even give a *firm* grip and add direct eye contact because they've been told that's how Westerners do it.

When do we exchange business cards?
Called *meishi* in Japanese, business cards are very important. The business card is more than a convenience. It represents one's personal identity, one's label, shingle, sign, rank, and name tag—all in one. (Incidentally, take care when listing your title on the card; make certain it is clear and accurate, neither overblown nor obscure. Also, have all the information printed in Japanese on the reverse side, preferably with the same quality printing on both sides lest you infer their language is second class.) In Japan, greetings and business cards go together like *sake* and rice. When exchanging business cards in Japan, the proper etiquette is:

- Exchange cards at the very first stages of an introduction.
- Present (and receive) the card with *both hands*. Grasp the card between thumbs and forefingers, with the lettering facing the recipient. Accompany all this with a slight bow. (See Figure 2.6.)
- Each recipient then takes several seconds to study the name, title, company name, and address before continuing.

Figure 2.6   In Japan, always present and receive business cards with both hands.

- *Now* . . . now shake hands, and bow a few more times.
- One final word of advice: Don't just casually stuff your new acquaintance's card into your pocket. Treat it with respect; it is, after all, a symbol of that person's very identity. Respectfully place the card on the table in front of you. Avoid writing notes on it, at least in front of the other person. That's tantamount to grabbing someone's name card off their lapel and scribbling all over it.

In his informative book *Japanese Etiquette & Ethics in Business*, (Passport Books, 1987), author Boye DeMente advises, "The lower the bow and the longer one holds the position, the stronger is the indication of respect, gratitude, sincerity, obeisance, humility, contriteness, etc." DeMente explains there are three degrees of bowing:

1. The informal bow (about 15 degrees, with the hands at the side) which is used for all casual occasions between people of all ranks;

2. The formal bow (30 degrees) with palms on knees, and often bobbing up and down; and

3. The formal or "highest form of salutation" that is rarely used and is reserved for the Imperial family. (So we won't detail it here!)

As a final reminder of the importance of rank in Japan, they actually joke among themselves that when playing golf it is customary to tee off in accordance with the level of their respective salaries.

Elsewhere in the Orient, in places like Taiwan, Hong Kong, Singapore, and mainland China, the bow is much less common. In those places, the conventional handshake is the customary form of greeting. You might detect a slight—very slight—bob of the head, but that's all.

Turning to other parts of the world, here are two more variations on the custom of shaking hands. In East Africa, friends shake hands with more of a casual light slap to each other's palm followed quickly by a cupping and grasping of fingers. And in Mexico, especially outside the metropolitan area of Mexico City, friends will greet with a conventional shaking of hands but then slip the palm upward and grasp each other's thumb.

A word of caution about the Thai *wai*, the Indian *namaste*, and Japanese bowing. While it is important to know, to practice, and to respect these forms of greetings, many people in the societies in which these greetings are practiced have traveled abroad, and may have adopted the handshake as the "lingua franca" of physical greeting. Wherever you travel, the handshake may greet you. Nevertheless, be prepared to demonstrate your knowledge and respect for the local customs as well. This show of respect will be appreciated.

(There are "amplifiers" or extensions to this set of actions we call greetings. These will be discussed elsewhere in the book. For example, the whole subject of *kissing lips, cheeks* and *hands* will be found in Chapter 3, under the appropriate sections on "lips" or "cheeks" or "hands.")

FAREWELLS

From greetings, we turn to *farewells*. The American goodbye wave can be interpreted in many parts of Europe and Latin America as the signal for "no." Cross cultural misunderstandings work both ways: When Italians motion "goodbye," it can be interpreted by Americans as the gesture for "come here." Let's examine more of these cross-cultural "goodbyes."

Americans tend to wave goodbye with the hand up, palm out, wrist stiff, and with a back-and-forth motion with the whole forearm and hand. (See Figure 2.7.) It is sometimes described as a "semaphore" action. In much of Europe, that gesture does not mean "goodbye" but, instead, signifies "no."

Figure 2.7   The American goodbye.

In Europe, the customary way to wave "hello" or "goodbye" is with the arm up and extended out, with the palm down, and just the hand bobbing up and down at the wrist (Figure 2.8).

In direct contrast, Italians and Greeks will often wave goodbye with the arm extended, *palm up*, curling all the fingers back and forth toward themselves. Most Americans interpret that gesture as meaning "come here." (See Figure 2.9.) Greeting and beckoning have gotten completely twisted around.

Figure 2.8   The European goodbye.

Figure 2.9 The Italian and Greek goodbye.

BECKONING

We now turn to the second group of common gestures—*beckoning gestures*. The way people beckon one another around the world can be almost as diverse as the way we greet and bid farewell to one another. (See Figure 2.10.)

Think about this commonplace situation for a moment: If you are seated in a restaurant and you wish to attract the attention of the waiter or waitress, what do you do? The odds are that whatever gesture you customarily use may be interpreted as strange or even rude in some other part of the globe.

Figure 2.10 Beckoning.

In the following discussion, we review a series of common beckoning gestures, and where they are popular, along with explanations of *other* meanings each gesture may have in other parts of the world.

In the United States, the common gesture for getting someone's attention, as when calling a waiter, is to raise a hand (with the index finger raised) about head high, or a little higher (Figure 2.11). It probably stems from our first experiences in school, where we are taught to simply raise our hand in order to get the teacher's attention. There are many variations.

The gesture in Figure 2.11 could be considered rude in some countries, like Japan, where pointing the finger at anyone is considered impolite.

In places like Germany, the signal as shown in Figure 2.11 also means "two", because two fingers (1 finger and a thumb) are being held upright. So an American might be signaling in this fashion and then saying "Waiter—some water, please," and a German waiter would bring two glasses of water.

Another beckoning or attention-getting motion common in the United States is to simply raise the hand and with the full, open palm wave the hand back and forth to attract attention.

The trouble with this motion is that in, say, Europe it could be interpreted as signaling "no." So, an American could be trying to get the attention of the waiter to come to his table and the waiter, seeing the gesture, says to himself: "That fellow is signaling 'no' to me. I guess he doesn't need me."

Also in America, a person might curl the index finger in and out to signal "come here."

Figure 2.11 The most common beckoning gesture in the United States.

In countries as wide-spread as Yugoslavia and Malaysia, that gesture is used only for calling *animals.* Therefore, using it to beckon a human would be terribly impolite.

In Indonesia and Australia, it is also used for beckoning "ladies of the night."

Throughout much of Europe and in many Latin American countries the preferred gesture for signaling "come over here" is to extend the arm, hand out, palm down, and then make a scratching motion with the fingers (Figure 2.12).

North Americans do not customarily use this gesture, and may consider it uncomfortable, effeminate, or puzzling.

If not done properly, in some European countries, particularly Italy and Greece, this gesture might be confused with one used to signal "goodbye." In that case, though, while the palm faces down, the fingers are *waggled* up and down as opposed to making an inward, scratching motion.

In France, the preferred way to call a waiter to your table is simply to catch his eye and then perhaps nod the head backwards quickly.

Figure 2.12   A beckoning gesture used in many European and Latin American countries.

In Colombia, one way to get a waiter's attention is to clap the hands lightly.

In China, to beckon a waiter to refill your tea, simply turn your empty cup upside down in its saucer. If the teapot is empty, turn its lid upside down. These gestures have no significance at all in most other countries.

In Spain, Mexico, Haiti and a sprinkling of other countries, when calling a waiter, restaurant patrons can be heard issuing a noise with the lips, something like "hssssst," or "pssssst." Another variation is to *snap the fingers.* But guidebooks caution that while this may be done by some local inhabitants, it is often considered impolite if done by visitors.

On one of my visits to Brazil, my group was seated in a fine restaurant with waiters scurrying busily around us so I used the opportunity to ask my dinner companions "What is the preferred way to get a waiter's attention in Brazil?" "Oh, we don't ever gesture or signal to get a waiter's attention," was the answer of my rather refined host. "In a fine restaurant, you should never have to call the waiter—he should hover so closely near your side that all you have to do is raise your head upward and whisper your wishes."

In Mexico I discovered perhaps the most unique way of beckoning a waiter. In some parts of the country they purse and pucker the lips and make a kissing noise with the lips. I would, however, in other countries urge you to exercise extreme caution in using this signal!

Try using this category of gestures to start your own investigation of various signals around the world. When you are visiting another country, and being hosted by local nationals at dinner, just ask "What is the customary way to beckon a waiter here?" It is an easy way to slip into a discussion of different gestures used around the world. And you may even discover a new beckoning gesture.

We now turn to the most delicate territory of all in the field of signals around the world: Insulting gestures.

INSULTING GESTURES

When it comes to flashing nonverbal *insults,* humans are clear, colorful, and creative—but sometimes contradictory.

Insulting gestures can be especially confusing because, as evidenced earlier in the incident between the American and German plastics engineers, some gestures you would use freely in front of your stodgy American Aunt Wilma would fry the hair of, say, your European Aunt Marie.

Figure 2.13 *Digitus impudicus.*

The "award" for the most ubiquitous and longest lived insulting gesture goes, as you may have suspected, to *"The Finger,"* hands down (pun intended). This gesture is performed by holding up the fist, knuckles facing outward, and extending the middle finger upward stiffly. It can simply be a static, frozen gesture or it can be accompanied by a thrusting or jerking motion upward (Figure 2.13).

Regardless of how this "single-digit salute" is amplified, it sends a powerful insulting message with little room for misunderstanding. And it has been that way for centuries. According to anthropologists, this gesture has been used for over 2,000 years. The Romans even had a special name for it, calling it *digitus impudicus* in Latin, or "impudent digit." Morris writes that "The (Roman) Emperor Caligula is thought to have used the extended middle finger when offering his hand to be kissed, as a deliberately scandalous act."

If Caligula were reincarnated to modern-day California, he could drive the highways there and instantly recognize that very same "scandalous" gesture. There it is sometimes called "the expressway digit" and used when an impatient, irate driver wishes to signal anger and frustration to another driver.

Arabs have modified this gesture in a peculiar way. For them the same insult is conveyed by extending the hand, palm down, fingers splayed outward, with the middle digit directed straight down (Figure 2.14).

The Soviets also have a variation. According to Tad Tuleja in his entertaining book *Curious Customs,* (Stonesong Press, 1987), the Russians bend back the middle finger of one hand with the

Figure 2.14   The Arab version of "The Finger."

forefinger of the other hand. It's called "looking under the cat's tail," a term that sounds as uninviting as it is rude.

Whether held up or down, the extended middle digit is generally regarded as a phallic symbol. In American slang, it sends a very strong and clear message. Another American label for this gesture is, curiously, "the bird," as in the phrase "So I flipped him the bird."

While the "impudent digit" is usually displayed openly and forcefully, it has also been used at least once to send a historic cryptic message. During the Korean Conflict, the U.S. Navy ship *Pueblo* was captured by North Koreans and the American crew held captive for many months. During their imprisonment, a photograph was taken of the crew and circulated by the North Koreans to show that the sailors were in good health. When the photo was taken, one of the crew surreptitiously displayed "the finger" in an attempt to signal defiance and indicate that the photo was a staged, insulting situation. The American press revealed this and, when the North Koreans learned of it, they severely punished the offender.

An enlarged version of the middle finger jerk is the *"forearm jerk"*, also called "the banana" in Brazil. Morris classifies this powerful and well-known gesture as a phallic symbol used mainly by men (Figure 2.15).

Again, the message is strong, sexual, and insulting. In American street lingo, it is yet another way to signal "Up yours!"

When issuing this gesture, there are several variations or levels of intensity. For example, in Yugoslavia a man may simply bend the arm at the elbow, make a fist (with knuckles away from

35

Figure 2.15   The forearm jerk.

his face) and shake the fist once (Figure 2.16). When I asked my guide in Dubrovnick "Exactly what does that gesture mean?", he looked at me, startled, and replied "What does it exactly mean?? It exactly means f—k you!"

In North America, Latin America and many parts of Europe, the "forearm jerk" is done using *both* arms in a clearly dynamic action: the right arm is bent at the elbow and the left hand then comes chopping down into the crook of the elbow while the fist of the right hand is jerked upward. For even greater emphasis and intensity, the left hand can also slap the *shoulder* of the right arm (Figure 2.17).

Figure 2.16   The Yugoslavian forearm jerk.

Figure 2.17   Forearm jerk, with emphasis!

Next on any listing of widespread and well-known insulting gestures might come a grouping called "animal insults." As a child, you probably used two of them to mock or taunt another child. They are the "ear waggle" and the "thumbing of the nose."

With the *"ear waggle,"* (Figure 2.18) the person places the hands at either side of the head, thumbs pointing inward at the temples or ears, and the other fingers spread. When one does this and flaps the hands back and forth, he is probably imitating the long, floppy ears of the donkey, an animal usually depicted as lazy and stupid.

"Thumbing the nose" involves placing the thumb of one hand on the tip of the nose with the other fingers splayed outward and

Figure 2.18   The "ear waggle."

Figure 2.19   "Thumbing the Nose."

then making a wiggling motion (Figure 2.19). Morris believes "This is thought to represent the hostile, erect comb of a fighting cock." There is another possible explanation, he says, and that is that it "relates to the ancient practice of imitating grotesque, long-nosed effigies."

While we seem to have a whole kaleidoscope of derisive gestures all over the world, these two are not only universally known but frequently used by young children everywhere. What swift, underground communication system causes them to learn these gestures at such an early age?

In contrast to the more universal insulting gestures used by many cultures, here are some specific, unique insulting gestures from individual countries.

- In France, If you play an imaginary flute, you are sending a signal saying "You are talking so long, I am getting bored."
- In Syria, picking the nose is a graphic signal to indicate "Go to hell!"
- In the United States, if a person imitates the action of shoveling, he is saying "This person (who is speaking) is creating a lot of manure."
- Among Jewish people, if one person points to his palm he is saying, in effect "Grass will grow on my palm before what I am hearing comes true."

Gestures for indicating that *someone*—or something—*is crazy* are legion. In the United States, one twirls the forefinger around the area of the temple or ear (which, in Argentina could be misinterpreted to mean "You have a telephone call").

In Germany, motorists who drive crazily may see nearby motorists put their forefingers to their temples and rotate them back and forth. So strong is this message and so insulting that one can possibly be arrested for it.

In Italy, whenever you see Italians tapping their hands to their forehead in a saluting manner, they are probably signaling the message that "You're *pazzo* (crazy)."

And take special care in Holland, where tapping the *temple* with the forefinger means someone is intelligent. But to indicate someone is considered stupid, the Dutch will tap the *forehead.* What a difference six inches can make.

One insulting gesture started one of the theater's best-known feuds. Here's the story.

In Elizabethan times, it was considered an insult to make a fist, place the thumbnail against the teeth, and then flick outward. William Shakespeare used this gesture in *Romeo and Juliet,* Act I, Scene I. When Sampson of the Capulet family flicks his thumb in this manner at Abram of the house of Montague, the Bard wrote "which is disgrace to them if they bear it." The Montagues reply with "Do you bite your thumb at us, sir?", and sword fighting ensues.

Another insulting gesture with deep historic roots is the *moutza* of Greece. This is known as the *"hand push."* At first glance, it merely looks like the person is holding his palm out toward you, as a traffic policeman might do to signal "Stop!" It is often

Figure 2.20   The Greek *moutza*.

accompanied by closing one eye and placing the other hand on the knee.

The *moutza* reaches back into ancient Greek history when fecal matter and dirt were hurled or pushed into the face of war prisoners. As a signal of insult, it survives with important implications even today. (See Figure 2.20.) A Western tourist visiting Greece might casually reject a vendor's plea with the hand, palm up and outward, and unknowingly be using an ugly signal as old as the Acropolis. And in West Africa this gesture means "You could have any one of five fathers!" which is another way of calling a person a "bastard."

Two other widespread insulting gestures involve the fist and the tongue. The *fist* gesture is a curious action because done one way, with the knuckles facing outward, it is a combative, threatening and aggressive gesture.

But, if the fist is rotated so the gathered fingers are displayed outward, it converts into a gesture of pride, power or victory.

The upraised fist, with the fingers outward, has become synonymous with the "Black Power" movement. History books show three separate scenes where this gesture has become memorialized: U.S. sprinter Tommie Smith at the 1968 Olympics in Mexico; Martin Luther King during his many protest marches; and Nelson

Mandela of South Africa on his triumphant 1990 tour of the United States and Europe. Each helped implant the concept of "Black Power" in the minds of the world.

Yet, with a mere 180-degree rotation of the forearm, wrist and hand, that fist gesture appears in the same history books with pictures showing rebellious crowds and angry demonstrators shaking their fists in unquestioned bellicosity.

Finally, let us turn to an assortment of what are considered ordinary, bland gestures in one society but which are insulting in others.

You will read more detail about each of these in pages that follow, so descriptions here will be brief:

- The "O.K." sign is terribly rude, even insulting, in diverse places like the Soviet Union, Germany, and Brazil. And, as you will learn later, in places like France and Japan it has entirely different meanings.

- The popular "V for victory" gesture, *in reverse* it could lead to painful consequences.

- The "vertical horns" gesture has a mixture of meanings, and one of them—in Italy—is very insulting.

- The "fig" gesture means "good luck" in Brazil but is terribly rude in Turkey.

- Even the "thumb's up" gesture is derogatory in some countries (e.g., Australia, Nigeria).

As a final demonstration of just how casual, innocent gestures in one society can actually be crude and insulting in another, imagine this scene:

> You are standing on a street corner, hands free of bundles or briefcases, whiling away the time in a free and happy mood. You swing your arms a bit, and casually smack the fist of one hand into the palm of the other. If you happen to be in places like Chile or France, you

Figure 2.21   The "innocent abroad," cheerful on a sunny after-noon, casually gestures, "Up Yours!"

> have just flashed to all those around you the equivalent
> of "Up Yours!" (Figure 2.21)

Often, when I relate this story, people react by saying "From now on, I'm just going to travel the world with my hands in my pockets." But in Japan, France, Belgium and a sprinking of other countries, standing with your hands in your pockets can be considered impolite.

The final general category of most popular gestures and body language might appropriately be called "The touchy subject of *touching.*"

TOUCHING

On my first trip to the Middle East, my Arab business contact and I toured the city, walking along the street visiting customers. He wore his long robe, the air was hot and dusty, a priest chanted the call to prayers from a nearby minaret, and I felt as far away from my American home as one could possibly be. At that moment, my business friend reached over, took my hand in his, and we continued walking along, his hand holding mine.

It didn't take me long to realize that something untoward was happening here, that some form of communication was being issued . . . but I didn't have the faintest idea what that message was. Also, I suddenly felt even farther from home.

Probably because I was so stunned, the one thing I didn't do was pull my hand away. I later learned that if I had jerked my hand out of his, I could have committed a Sahara-sized *faux pas.* In his country, this act of taking my hand in his was a sign of great friendship and respect.

That was my first lesson about space relationships between different people. I quickly learned that it was a world of extremes—important extremes—with some cultures seeking bodily contact and others studiously avoiding it. Ken Cooper, in his book *Nonverbal Communication For Business Success* (AMACOM, NY 1979), writes that he once covertly observed conversations in outdoor cafes in several different countries and counted the number of casual touches (of self or of the other party) per hour. The results: San Juan, Puerto Rico, 180 per hour; Paris, 110 per hour; Florida, 2 per hour; London, 0 per hour.

I also learned that the Middle East was not the only region where it is quite acceptable for two men to walk cradling an elbow, arm-in-arm, or even holding hands. Korea, Indochina, Greece, and Italy are also regarded as "touch–oriented" countries. Such physical displays in those countries usually signal friendship. Touching between men—often seen as an indication of homosexuality in North America—is quite the opposite. In some of the most "touch–oriented" areas homosexuality is coldly rejected.

Here, on a scale of "touch" or "don't touch," is a geographic measuring stick:

Don't Touch	*Touch*
Japan	Middle East countries
United States & Canada	Latin countries
England	Italy
Scandinavia	Greece
Other Northern	Spain & Portugal
European countries	Some Asian countries
Australia	Russia
Estonia	

Middle Ground
France
China
Ireland
India

43

Can the casual act of touching be all that important? The answer is "yes"—important enough to make bold headlines in at least one country's national newspapers:

> When Queen Elizabeth paid one of her periodic visits to Canada, a Canadian provincial transport minister escorted her through a crowd by gently touching her elbow; he may have even touched the small of her back. Newspaper headlines in England screamed protests: "Hands off our Queen," said one; "Row Over Man Who Touched Queen," read another.

The reason behind that uproar was that it is an unwritten rule among the British that no one touches the Queen. Even when shaking hands, the rule is that she must make the first move.

In the United States, office workers and school teachers are warned and trained to avoid any casual touching of their employees or students. A university professor of communications explains that "an innocuous touch on someone's hand or arm can be misconstrued as a sexual move, especially if we let it linger." Unwanted touching in U.S. business offices can lead to law suits for sexual harassment while teachers may be accused of molestation if they frequently hug, pat, or touch their students.

Yet there are strange contradictions, especially in the United States. Here are two examples:

> I once asked an audience of U.S. businessmen what they would do if they boarded a crowded airplane, sat next to a large man and found themselves pressing elbows, maybe even shoulders and upper arms as well, throughout the whole trip. "Nothing," was the consensus. "It happens all the time," they agreed. I countered, "Well, what would you do then if that same man then touched your knee with his hand?" The reaction was unanimous: "Move the knee." "And," one added, "if, God forbid, he *grabbed* my knee, I would punch him in the nose."

> The second contradiction regarding rules for touching occurs on elevators and subways. As we learned in Chapter 1, on a crowded elevator or an underground train at commuting time, people will stand shoulder-to-shoulder, arm-to-arm, and accept such rubbing of shoulders without complaint. But, the rule is "Touch *only* from shoulder to elbow. No other parts of the body."

Cultures are colliding every day over this dilemma of "to touch or not to touch." In New York City, Korean immigrants in recent years have started new lives by opening retail shops of all kinds. But, when American customers make a purchase and receive their change, the Korean merchants place the money on the counter to avoid any physical contact. "They won't touch my hand," one customer noticed. "They won't even place coins in my hand. It's somewhat cold and insulting. And furthermore, they won't look me in the eyes."

One Korean merchant explained in a national television interview that in his homeland they are taught to avoid physical contact of any kind. The same with direct eye contact. "We are taught that either gesture could have sexual connotations," he added, "so we carefully avoid them."

And here's a surefire way for a North American to make a Japanese acquaintance feel uncomfortable. Just go up and place your arm around him, as you would a college buddy or big brother. Even though the Japanese permit themselves to be jammed into subways and trains, they are not regarded as a touching society. To explain this, anthropologist Edward T. Hall says the Japanese handle any unease about being packed into public places by averting eyes, avoiding eye contact, drawing within themselves and thus "touching without feeling."

Closely related to the societal customs of touching is that of spatial relationships. Anthropologists tell us that each of us walks around inside "bubbles of personal space." The size of the bubble represents our personal territory, territorial imperative, or "personal buffer zones." We neither like nor tolerate it when someone invades our bubble. We become distinctly uncomfortable.

But as we travel to different places around the world, we learn that some cultural bubbles are larger or smaller than others. Here is a ruler for measuring the bubbles between nationalities:

- The American "bubble" extends about 12 to 15 inches, and so we may stand a combined 24 to 30 inches apart. Scientists point out this just happens to be an arm's length away (which carries a certain symbolism, doesn't it?). Anthropologist George Renwick says "When two Americans stand facing one another in any normal social or business situation, one could stretch out his arm and put his thumb in the other person's ear."

- Orientals, and especially the Japanese, stand even farther apart, Renwick adds. When it comes to ordinary business or social situations, they have the largest bubbles of all. However, as we have learned, in their own public settings, where crowding is impossible to avoid, they accept body contact or just seem to ignore it by "retreating within themselves."

- Latins and Middle Easterners, on the other hand, stand much closer than Americans. They may stand, literally, toe-to-toe. They may even place a hand on the other's forearm or elbow, or finger the lapel of the other person.

Americans claim it takes years of experience, plus steely resolve, to stand that close and smell that many breaths. Some observers in Latin America even have a name for this charade. They call it "the conversational tango." That's the "dance" done by an American or European freshly arrived in Latin America who is confronted by this sudden and startling custom of closeness. The first reaction of the visitor is to step backward. But the Latin will follow. So, the visitor steps back again. The Latin follows. And so it goes, in a poorly choreographed tango (Figure 2.22). As one observer put it, "The dance stops only when the American is backed into a corner."

But even as these words are written, touch codes are changing all over the world. In the United States, politicians have

Figure 2.22   The first step in a conversational tango.

learned the value of touch. They frequently give two-handed handshakes, casually touch the elbow of another, or lightly touch the back of the person standing next to them. "Pressing flesh" has become a byword on political campaigns. Also, Japanese managers posted in U.S. factories are steeling themselves and learning to accept finger-crunching handshakes, back patting, and maybe even a friendly arm around the shoulder for the softball team photo.

The "hugging professor," Leo Buscaglia, tours cities and campuses presenting captivating lectures on the joy of hugging. His popular books and video and audio tapes make his audiences realize that separateness and aloofness can be a lonely, cold existence.

Finally, in Helen Colton's wonderful book, *The Gift of Touch*, she describes how Swedish actress Liv Ullman was once touring famine-stricken lands on behalf of UNICEF. In Bangladesh, after a warm visit with a woman there, Ullman gave the woman a hug. But she felt the woman suddenly draw away. Through her interpreter, Ullman asked why. The woman answered, "In my country, we kiss feet when we say goodbye." Ullman, the quintessential lady, unhesitatingly bent down and kissed the woman's feet. Then they hugged, each woman having exchanged the parting ritual of her own world.

We now turn to four specific and common gestures. Each of these is used and known in a large number of societies—but, as you will see, each gesture has different meanings attached to it depending on the locale.

THE "O.K." SIGN

In the 1950s, then Vice-President Richard Nixon made a goodwill tour of Latin America. At that time, there was already widespread hostility toward the United States and Nixon unwittingly added fuel to the fires of resentment with a single, unthinking act. At one of his early stops, Nixon stepped off his airplane and flashed the "A-O.K." sign to the waiting crowd. They responded by booing. In addition, newspapers the next day published large photographs of Nixon and his gesture. Why was it headline news? Because in their culture, what Nixon had signalled was the gesture equivalent for "Screw you!" (Figure 2.23.)

A Frenchman, particularly in the South of France, would read that very same gesture as meaning "zero" or "worthless." I once took a hotel room in France and when the concierge asked "Is your room satisfactory?" I replied with the "O.K." sign. With a

Figure 2.23

shrug of irritation, the concierge said, "If you don't like it, we'll just have to find you another room."

In Japan, the thumb and forefinger making a circle is used as a symbol for money—the fingers creating the round outline of a coin. For example, when a Japanese buys a newspaper or soft drink and wants the change in coins, he or she might flash this gesture.

Because of this use, the gesture could have serious consequences when incorrectly used. Imagine a Western businessperson who has negotiated a contract with a Japanese and, at the conclusion, casually makes the "O.K." sign and says: "Fine. Let's sign the contract." The Japanese might say to himself "Oh! He's giving me the sign for 'money.' Is he saying he wants some money to sign? Is he asking for a bribe?"

The connections between this gesture and coins, zero and anatomy are clearer than how and why this gesture means "O.K." In American Sign Language for the deaf, the thumb-and-finger-circle designates the letter "O," but the other three fingers on the hand are cupped as well. Also, the letter "K" is made by making a "V" with the index and middle fingers. So, our "O.K." sign apparently does not come from that source.

The spoken term for "O.K." probably originated in the United States in 1840. At that time, the Democratic party's "Old Kinderhook" label was given to its presidential candidate Martin Van Buren, who was born in Kinderhook, N.Y. As a campaign slogan, this was shortened to "O.K. Van Buren." One supposition might be that the circle signals the letter "O" and the other three outstretched fingers are a crude replica of the letter "K," but the exact origin is unclear.

A very crude variation on this gesture is to form a circle with the thumb and forefinger of one hand and then poke the forefinger of the other hand through the circle. In many locales, this is considered an obscene way to signal the act of coitus.

Clearly, the "O.K." gesture as Americans and many others know it, is "non-O.K." when landing in other lands and communicating among other cultures. Better, perhaps, to quickly learn the words in the local language for "Yes" and "Fine" and keep your hands at your side.

THUMBS UP GESTURE

Pilots do it the world over. Astronauts and cosmonauts even do it out of this world. It has become an almost universal signal for "Everything's O.K." or "Fine" or "Good Going!" and a dozen other messages along that vein.

But, watch out! There are some exceptions—important exceptions. Before we get to those, however, let's review the origins of the gesture.

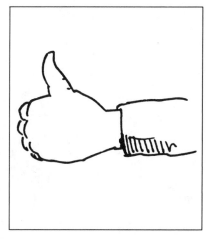

Origins, according to Hollywood's portrayal, go back to the gladiators of Rome who received the "thumbs up" signal from the emperor who thought that a courageous gladiator should live, or "thumbs down" which signaled the opposite, a bloody death sentence for the losing warrior.

Once again, Hollywood may be guilty of creating its own history.

Desmond Morris suggests that there are no ancient references to this symbol. He contends that recent historians may have misunderstood the Latin phrase *pollice verso* to mean a "down-turned thumb." That bit of Latin means instead, according to him, "a turned thumb," one that is moved in some unspecified way. No direction was specified. Morris theorizes that the ancient Romans would extend their thumbs in some fashion when they wished to signal death. Furthermore, he contends that to signal "he shall live" they would tuck their thumb inside their fist.

Whatever the origin—Hollywood or history—the thumbs up gesture is now well-known throughout North America and much of Europe. It is perhaps least known in Greece and Italy, but even there it has been imported and observed (although not widely). The same is true in the Far East where it is largely imported and known as a Western gesture.

In the United States and parts of Europe, the "Thumbs-Up" gesture is commonly used to signal that one is hitch-hiking. In Nigeria, however, as we learned in an incident related in Chapter 1, it is viewed as a rude gesture. Foreigners traveling in Nigeria have innocently tried hitch-hiking only to be roughed up for appearing to be sending insults to passing motorists.

In the "Down Under" country, posing the "Thumbs-Up" gesture might just get you "Down and Out." In Australia, flashing the upright thumb and then making a slight jerk upward is generally used to silently signal "Up Yours!" (Figure 2.24.)

Figure 2.24   The "innocent abroad" in Australia tries to close the deal . . . with "Up Yours!"

If you like *counting* with your fingers, be cautious as you travel abroad because you might just add up to total confusion. In Germany, for example, to signal "one" a person uses the upright thumb instead of the forefinger. Therefore, in a German *gasthaus* beer garden, to order "one beer" you would flash the "Thumbs-Up" gesture. Many Westerners use the *forefinger* to signal "one," more or less ignoring the thumb. But, do that in Germany— casually hold up the forefinger and forget the thumb—and it could be seen as meaning "two," with the result that you'd be drinking two beers instead of one.

In Japan, they use the fingers to count visually just as most cultures do. However, in Japan counting *begins* with the index finger (not the thumb) to designate "one"; then the index and middle fingers combined equal "two"; the combination of index, middle and ring fingers is "three," and adding the little finger equals "four." Then the Japanese show the upright thumb alone to mean "five." So, if you order "One beer" with your thumb in Japan you may well receive five beers.

When one thinks about it, the thumb is a wonderfully versatile and utilitarian digit. Artists hold it in front of their eyes, peering over it to gain a sense of perspective and depth. We like to put people "under our thumb," and film critics and editorial writers frequently use "thumbs up" or "thumbs down" to indicate approval or rejection, respectively. Finally, we "thumb our noses," bite our thumb to hurl an insult à la Shakespeare, suck our thumbs as infants, and if that is not sufficient, there must be at least a million "rules of thumb."

So the thumb becomes a valuable part of our daily worldwide communication, whether in school to ridicule a schoolmate with the "nose thumb" or in space to reassure a spacemate with the "thumbs-up" gesture.

Just be careful where you point your thumb in places like Nigeria and Australia.

"V" FOR VICTORY

Since World War II, followed by the Peace Movement of the 1960s, holding two fingers upright has signaled "Victory" or "Peace" for millions of people.

But in England, where it probably originated, an innocent twist of the wrist could result in a jolt in the nose. There, if the *palm and fingers face inward,* it means "Up yours!" especially if executed with an upward jerk of the fingers (Figure 2.25).

**Figure 2.25   The "innocent abroad" befriends a Britisher . . .
with "Up Yours!"**

I once had the pleasure of appearing on the Merv Griffin
late-night television show. I demonstrated that "V for victory"
flashed with the fingers and palm *outward* was fine. But then I
asked Griffin, "But in England do you know what it means if
you turn the hand around?" "Oh, I bet I know," Griffin said
quickly. "It's like 'the finger' only *double*. It's like saying 'And
here's one for your mother, too!'"

A more plausible story about the origin of the rude version of
this gesture was supplied to me by a military historian in England.
Five hundred years ago, English bowmen were considered as
destructive as today's nuclear weapons. Consequently, if such a
bowman were captured, the French reportedly cut off the forefinger and middle finger of the hand that drew the bowstring.
That had the effect of disarming the English archer for life.

After the battles of Agincourt and Crecy, so the story goes,
where the French were heavily defeated by the expert English
archers, the surviving French were marched off the battlefield to
the taunts of the victorious English. The English added further
insult to the French by holding up their hands, forefinger and
middle finger stiffly upright, palms inward, to show both fingers
fully intact.

Winston Churchill may have known this historic tidbit because he adopted the "V" as a courageous gesture in World War
II. It became so identified with him that contemporary statues and
history books frequently show him proudly displaying that gesture. But, we should note, with the palm facing *outward*, and
therefore not the insult the English bowmen flashed at the French.

Other historians might argue that Churchill adopted that signal only after a Belgian radio announcer, Victor De Lavelaye, popularized the opening notes of Beethoven's "Fifth Symphony," which in Morse Code was the signal for the letter "V." Thus, according to this version, the *sound* came first, then the "V" in Morse Code, and *then* Churchill adopted it as his visual signature.

Today French, Americans, and other nationalities are seen presenting the "V for victory" or "Peace" signal . . . but unknowingly flashing it *either* way, palm out or palm in. Most are not aware that when visiting England one of those versions could very possibly result in a reaction far removed from "Peace." In fact, the result might possibly be an English bloody, bloody nose.

Even President George Bush has provided a quip on the various origins and meanings of the "V" signal. While jogging one morning, according to news reports he flashed the "V" signal and mischievously asked journalists accompanying him "Do you know what this means? It's Julius Caesar ordering five beers."

VERTICAL HORNS, OR "HOOK 'EM HORNS"

For thousands of avid Texas football fans, this is the time-honored rallying gesture for the University of Texas "Longhorn" football team.

Export it to Italy, however, and this gesture gets twisted around like a plate of spaghetti. For millions of Italians it is the *cornuto,* and it signifies an entirely different meaning. It says "You are being cuckolded!" In more kindly terms, one person is signaling to the other that "Your spouse is being unfaithful." (See Figure 2.26.) That's a far cry from "hook 'em horns" and resulted in this actual incident.

John C. Givens Jr., an officer ir U.S. Army Intelligence stationed in Italy, reported that American soldiers from Texas were in a nightclub one evening when they

Figure 2.26   In Italy, the "innocent abroad," a Texas football fan . . . gets sidelined!

> discovered that several other G.I.s present were also from the state of Texas. They started signaling the Texas "hook 'em horns" gesture between them. But, Italian waiters and other locals misunderstood and took immediate offense. What started as a friendly reunion ended up as a room-clearing brawl.

There are different theories about how and why "horns" have become associated with the insult of cuckoldry. One of them is that they taunt impotence and stupidity.

But, once again, here is an example of the *ying/yang* in gestures. Where it may signal deception and stupidity in Italy, in Brazil and Venezuela making horns with the fingers is a sign for good luck! You can actually buy talismans in this shape for necklaces and charm bracelets.

There are other variations, as well. When these same two fingers are pointed *at* someone, it can signify that either "the evil eye" or a "curse" is being placed on someone. This is the case in some African countries, where this gesture directs or places a curse. (See Figure 2.27.)

In Italy, replicas of hands showing the "horns" can be found in shop windows as a means of warding off evil spirits. The same is true in Malta, where fishing boats may be seen with the hands in the "horn" position painted on them as a hope for avoiding evil mishaps.

For still another interpretation, consider this. When I was a child in my home state of Wisconsin, my buddies and I used this

Figure 2.27   An African curse.

very same gesture, but to us it meant neither the evil eye or good luck. Instead we were saying "Bull—!" or, putting it more literally, "You're full of horse manure."

In American baseball, when a player holds up his hand with these two fingers upright he is signaling to his teammates that "There are two outs. Only one more to end this inning."

Among three other widely separate cultures, it is considered a sign for cattle. Hindu dancers employ it to represent a bovine. An American Indian might do the same, or place his fingers on his temples, pointing them inward, to represent bison. And an Australian Aborigine would do almost the same gesture as sign language for the term "cattle."

An entirely different meaning is given to this signal among Satanic cults in America. Members of this cult use it as a "recognition sign" and, among that coterie, it signifies the horns of the Devil.

There we have it: One single hand gesture—a handful of different meanings. Depending on where it is used, it can mean: a college rallying sign, a signal of infidelity, a voodoo-like curse, a symbol for "Good Luck," the Devil, or "You're full of horse apples."

Finally, in Milwaukee, Wisconsin, home of numerous foundries and metal–punching factories, coarse barroom humor gives it still a different meaning. "In our taverns," Milwaukeeans explain, "when you see someone hold his hand up like that with only the two outward fingers standing upright, it simply means that a veteran, long-suffering punch press operator is ordering four beers."

55

3

Gestures:
Head to Toe

This chapter presents a *catalog of gestures* arranged by body part, starting at the head and moving down the length of the body, as follows:

Head and Face

Eyes

Ears

Nose

Cheeks

Lips and Mouth

Chin

Arms

Hands

Fingers

Legs and Feet

Full Body

If you are curious about a particular gesture you have observed, first determine which part of the body plays the most important role. Is it the head? The hands? Then turn to that section in this chapter and scan the headings and illustrations for the gesture you had in mind. You will find some duplications where gestures involve more than one part of the body.

HEAD AND FACE

The head and face are the most expressive and impressive parts of the body. Our faces are capable of showing anger, pain, joy, shock, sorrow, confidence, exhaustion, surprise, suspicion, bewilderment, boredom, cunning, doubt, and more. The face can pout, grimace, snarl, wince, blush, blanch, gape, smirk, glare, or frown. The head can nod, shake, jerk, tilt, bob, waggle, thrust, duck, turn, and even shiver.

We send scores of messages each day using just the head and face. Pantomimists learn them all. The late comedian, movie star, and storyteller, Danny Kaye, traveled the world enchanting audiences of children with his stories, while never knowing or speaking one word of their language.

And then there is the smile. A Wayne State University researcher claims that there are some 1,814,400 different kinds of smiles. While that may seem far-fetched, consider that just one of those smiles has been mystifying art lovers for centuries: the Mona Lisa smile. The true meaning behind her smile remains an enigma.

The head and face are wonderfully versatile instruments for communications. Here are some examples.

As we all know, *nodding the head* up and down signals "yes," and shaking it back and forth means "no." Elementary. We all send messages this way every day (Figure 3.1). But consider these contradictions:

In Bulgaria, parts of Greece, Yugoslavia, Turkey, Iran, and Bengal it is *the reverse*. There, nodding the head up and down means "no." And shaking the head back and forth means "yes." (If you've got that, now shake your head back and forth—"yes.")

Another variation occurs in Greece. There, tipping the head back rather abruptly (or, jerking the chin up) while raising the eyebrows means "no." To indicate "yes" in Greece, drop the chin down several times.

Still another variation involves the nod backwards accompanied by a clicking of the tongue. In Saudi Arabia, Greece, Bulgaria, and some other parts of the Middle East, this means "no."

In Greece, tilting the whole head from side-to-side laterally means "no."

Confused? So were the Russians who occupied Bulgaria in the nineteenth century. Respecting local customs, Russian soldiers tried to discipline themselves to nod up and down when

Figure 3.1 Nodding and shaking the head mean different things to different people.

they meant "no" and to shake their heads when they wanted to signal "yes." The problem was that the Bulgarians never knew if the Russians were "speaking" in Bulgarian or their own language, so the use of head signals for communications broke down.

Charles Darwin theorized that both movements mimic infantile nursing patterns: The forward head nod is seen as part of the breast-seeking or breast-accepting pattern, and the head–shaking gesture is a sign of refusal.

The *tossing the head* backward negation gesture of Greece is also used in Southern Italy, Malta, and Tunisia (Figure 3.2). But in Germany and Scandinavia it becomes a beckoning motion. And in India, it means "yes." With remote groups like the Maoris in New Zealand, the Tagals of the Philippines, and the Dyaks of Borneo, it means "yes" as in "Yes, of course."

Tapping the head with the forefinger has a variety of meanings, some of them opposites (Figure 3.3). In Argentina and Peru it can mean "I'm thinking." If the tapping is done near the temple, it can mean "That's very intelligent." Yet in North America and other places, it can either mean "that person is very intelligent," or "that person is tetched, crazy." It all depends on the statement accompanying the gestures. In Holland, if the finger is tapped to the *center of the forehead*, it means "He's crazy."

Covering the head is a requirement for Jewish men and women in conservative or orthodox synagogues, for women entering certain Catholic religious shrines, and for Muslim women in public places at all times. According to the protocol of Catholicism, when women meet the Pope they must wear a shawl or other covering on their heads.

Figure 3.2   Tossing the head backward.

Figure 3.3   The meaning of a tap on the head can depend on where you tap.

Slapping the hand to the back of the head is, according to author and anthropologist David Givens, an automatic gesture done by most cultures and designates being disturbed or startled. Other anthropologists report some Bolivian Indian tribes indicate both anger and joy by slapping the back of the head.

Rocking the head slowly, back and forth, side-to-side, is a gesture used in India and means "Yes, I am listening." At first observation, Westerners confuse this as meaning "No."

Scratching the head is a gesture occurring all over the world and thought to be almost instinctive. It signals "I am confused" or "I am skeptical."

(There are many gestures involving the head in conjunction with the hands or fingers. Where these are predominantly motions involving the hands or fingers, they will be found later in this chapter under the sections devoted to that part of the body.)

EYES

"Look me in the eye, son" is a command that's been repeated countless times through the centuries in every corner of the map. But, as we will quickly learn here, some cultures are much more eye–oriented than others.

American, Canadian, British, Eastern European, and Jewish cultures favor "face-to-face" relationships. Hispanic women may often hold eye contact longer than others, even with strange men. But many Orientals, Puerto Ricans, West Indians and African Americans tend to avoid such direct eye contact.

In one region of Africa, a U.S. Peace Corps volunteer upset tribal elders because of her teaching practices. The woman required her students to look her in the eye. In that particular culture, it was not permissible for a child to look an adult in the eye. Much the same is true among Native Americans. It is impolite to look a senior person straight in the eyes; respect is shown by avoiding the eyes.

In Japan, Korea, and Thailand, it is considered rude to stare. Prolonged direct eye contact is considered impolite and even intimidating. A few shrewd Japanese negotiators have learned that Westerners expect averted eyes, so at the bargaining tables the Japanese do *just the opposite.* They sit and stare. This is so atypical of the Japanese that it can completely unnerve Westerners and cause them to disclose their next compromise.

In Saudi Arabia, one is expected to maintain strong eye contact because of the adage "the eyes are the windows to the soul." However, when doing this, visitors often become concerned by the languid, or half-shut, appearance of the eyes of many Mid-Easterners which should not be interpreted as disinterest.

The *eyebrows* can signal several different emotions. Those two lines of facial hair can indicate anger, confusion, openness, curiosity, and even flirtation (Figure 3.4).

When humans are alerted, the pupils are dilated and the eyebrows are raised. When threatened or angry, humans lower the eyebrows. In Peru, raising the eyebrows can mean "money" or "Pay me." In Tonga, it would mean "Yes," or "I agree."

The *eyebrow flash* is, in America and elsewhere, a sign of flirtation used by men when they see a pretty girl. It may have been popularized by the 1930s film star Groucho Marx, noted for

Figure 3.4   Variations of *the eyebrow flash.*

Figure 3.5   The single eyelid wink.

his heavily painted eyebrows which he repeatedly flashed up and down while leering at pretty women.

Wetting the little finger and drawing it across the *eyebrow* is a signal sometimes used among men in the United States to indicate that some other person is homosexual. It mimics the feminine action of applying eyebrow makeup.

Blinking the eyes can also have meaning, depending on the culture. In Taiwan and Hong Kong, repeatedly blinking the eyes at someone is considered impolite.

Among Americans and Europeans, *winking* with one eyelid signifies some shared secret, yet it is regarded as impolite in Hong Kong (Figure 3.5). In the United States, it is also a rather bold, flirtatious gesture, but in Australia it is improper to wink at women.

The *eyelid pull* (pulling a corner of one eye down with the index finger) conveys "alertness," but with several related variations (Figure 3.6). For example, in places like England and France it means "You can't fool me. I see what you're up to." But in Italy, it means "Be careful. Pay attention. Keep your eyes peeled." There, it may also hint "Be careful—he's a crook." And in Yugoslavia it can mean sadness or disappointment, as if a tear is falling. It might be used, for example, by one tour guide signaling to a colleague that "I got no tip from this tourist."

Rolling the eyes is a fairly common gesture around the world, and suggests incredulity or amazement.

Closed eyes do not necessarily indicate boredom or sleep. In Japan, as we learned in the incident with the Governor and the American businessman visiting Japan (page 13), it may be used when a Japanese listener is in deep concentration.

Figure 3.6   The eyelid pull.

EARS

The *earlobe flick* may be seen in Italy where touching or holding or tugging or flicking the earlobe signifies that some other person is effeminate or homosexual (Figure 3.7). It probably stems from the feminine habit of wearing earrings.

The *ear grasp* in India is a sign of apology, as when a servant drops a dish or commits some other error (Figure 3.8).

In Brazil, *pinching the earlobe* with the thumb and forefinger is a way of expressing appreciation, as when you wish to signal you have enjoyed a meal. Some Brazilians, to add further

Figure 3.7   The earlobe flick.

Figure 3.8   The ear grasp.

emphasis, will reach around over the top of the head and grasp the opposite earlobe.

Cupping the ear with one hand is understood almost universally to mean "I can't hear you."

Rotating the forefinger around in front of the ear has two entirely different meanings: in the United States, it usually connotes that someone or something is "crazy"; yet in Argentina, it can be a signal to indicate "You have a telephone call." (See Figure 3.9.)

In the United States, the customary way to signal "You have a telephone call" is *holding an imaginary telephone to the ear.* A slight amplification on this motion is to hold the hand near the ear and

Figure 3.9   Either you're crazy or you have a phone call.

stiffly extend the thumb and little finger outward as if to emulate the shape of a phone receiver.

NOSE

Sticking one's nose into someone else's business is only one way to communicate with the nose. It can also be tapped, circled, thumbed, wiggled, pushed, scratched, or twisted, and each action signals a meaningful message.

The *nose tap* can be seen in England and in Italy, but the meaning is slightly different in each locale (Figure 3.10). In England it probably means confidentiality, as in "Don't spread this around," or "Let's keep this between us only." On the other hand, in Italy it is more of a friendly warning: "Watch out. Take care."

The *nose circle* may be seen in Colombia and is made by forming a circle with the thumb and forefinger and placing it over the nose (Figure 3.11). In Colombia, it signals that the person in question is homosexual.

Making a *"V" over the nose* with the forefinger and middle finger with the palm inward toward the face, is obscene in such disparate places as Saudi Arabia and Mexico (Figure 3.12). This gesture transforms the tip of the nose into a symbolic phallus.

Thumbing the nose is an almost universally known insulting gesture (Figure 3.13). It is often used by children (and others!) who want to mock one another with derision. Added emphasis comes when two hands are joined in tandem. (See the section on "Insulting Gestures" in Chapter 2 for more information.)

Figure 3.10   The nose tap.

Figure 3.11   The nose circle.

The nose twist is apparently totally unique to France. There it signifies drunkenness and may be used by one person signaling to a second person that a third party has become drunk. (See Figure 3.14.)

Wiggling the nose, in Puerto Rico, asks the question "What's going on?" (In other countries it probably just means the nose-wiggler has an itch.)

Wrinkling the nose in the United States and many other countries is an indication of disgust, as expressed in the phrases "I don't like that," or "I'm disgusted." It can also pose the question "What's that smell?"

Figure 3.12   A Saudi obscenity.

Figure 3.13   Thumbing the nose.

Holding the nose with thumb and forefinger is a fairly universal and well-understood sign that says "Something smells bad." In Hollywood, it has the distinctive meaning that the product viewed is a flop.

Scratching or rubbing the side of the nose can, according to author and anthropologist Julius Fast, be an unconscious signal that someone is telling a lie. "Watch politicians when they speak, and if they stroke the side of their nose with their forefinger it usually means 'I'm going to say something outrageous . . . or I'm telling a bare-faced lie.'"

Figure 3.14   Oo-la-la! A jug of wine, a jug of wine, and thou.

CHEEKS

This part of the body has been memorialized metaphorically in the Bible with the admonishment to "turn the other cheek." That gesture of forgiveness is urged when one is offended or injured by an adversary. On the other hand, the British call someone "cheeky" if they are impudent, bold, or brassy.

The *cheek screw* is primarily an Italian gesture of praise, as when observing a pretty girl. Here the extended forefinger is rotated, or turned into the cheek (Figure 3.15). It is rarely seen or understood—with this meaning—outside of Italy. In Germany, it has an entirely different message: "That's crazy."

A variation on this gesture would be to press the thumb and forefinger together and twist them into the cheek. Again seen only in italy, it would mean "attractive" or "good" or "pretty."

The *cheek stroke* in Greece, Italy and Spain means "attractive," and would be one way of signaling "I see a pretty girl." In Yugoslavia, it signifies "success." In the United States, it can also be a sign of contemplation, as if saying "That's interesting—let me think about that." In a scattering of other countries, it can mean "ill" or "thin." This gesture can be done with the thumb and other fingers stroking each side of the face, or with just the thumb and forefinger stroking downward on either side of the face. (See Figure 3.16.)

Cheek-kissing is not as simple as it may sound. In places like Russia, and perhaps the Middle East, they actually *kiss* the cheek. In other places—like France or Italy or throughout Latin America—it is considered "kissing the air." That means cheeks touch

Figure 3.15   The cheek screw.

Figure 3.16   The cheek stroke.

and the lips make the sound of kissing, but the lips don't actually press against the cheek.

For the uninitiated, the quandary becomes "How many times does one kiss? Once? Or on both cheeks?" In the countries of Latin America in which cheek-kissing is practiced, only one cheek is usually kissed. In places like France, they may kiss twice (once on each cheek). And in Belgium and Russia, they may kiss three times—one side, then the other, and back to the first side.

But even before the one-two-three quandary comes the more basic question "How do you know when to kiss cheeks and when not to? When am I expected to buss and when not?" The answer comes from a slight tugging with the hand. As you shake hands with someone, if that other person believes she (or he) knows you well enough, you may feel a slight pulling on your hand. That's the signal to move in (go to *your* left, otherwise you'll bump noses) and press cheeks. One seasoned world traveler comments, "You'll quickly learn when a woman acquaintance expects you to kiss her cheek—she just reels you in with her hand."

LIPS AND MOUTH

Our lips and mouth send not only verbal signals but a whole collection of nonverbal communiques. We pout, whistle, yawn, smile, bite, point, sneeze, and spit—each sending its own special unspoken message.

But the winner as the strongest lip-mouth communicator of all is the *kiss*.

Tennis great Bjorn Borg kissed his newly won Wimbledon trophy, and mothers around the world kiss their children's bruises to "make them better." The Iraqi POWs kissed the hands of their Allied Coalition captors to show their humbled state. In the United States, childhood friends but professional basketball opponents Ervin "Magic" Johnson and Isaiah Thomas startled the sports world by kissing one another at the beginning of a nationally televised championship playoff game.

So important is the kiss that we speak figuratively of "the kiss of death," and the act of mouth-to-mouth resuscitation is called "the kiss of life."

The French . . . well, the French seem to be doing it everywhere all the time: on the cheeks, the hands, and even into the air. So serious do the French take kissing that two of them (Xavier Fauche and Christiane Noetzin) once wrote a 294-page book titled, simply, *Le Baiser* (*The Kiss*). One of the most famous sculptures in the world, "The Kiss," was done by a Frenchman, Auguste Rodin in 1886.

Hollywood has made the kiss into a *geste supreme,* with Cary Grant and Ingrid Bergman holding the record for the longest and most passionate kiss ever screened in the film "Notorious." Henry Fonda and Katherine Hepburn popularized a whole new term for it in their film "On Golden Pond" when they referred to kissing as "suck face."

Then there is "deep kissing" or "deep-tongue kissing." That's when it might be said we "talk with tongues." The French (of course, the French) had a kissing game in the 19th century called *maraichinage* which involved deep-tongue kissing between at least ten or more couples who changed partners weekly. In some parts of France, this "tongue dueling" was conducted in parks and even in churches. It was banned by the clergy in 1864.

For the scientific origin of deep kissing, Desmond Morris writes that it derives from when primitive women weaned their babies by passing chewed-up food mouth-to-mouth.

Today, in the Orient, kissing is considered an intimate sexual act and not permissible in public, even as a social greeting.

Figure 3.17   More than just a polite greeting?

Among the Tapuya of South America, however, kisses are exchanged *only* among the males as a sign of peace.

Making a kissing *sound* is a multi-meaning gesture. In Mexico, it is used to beckon a waiter in a restaurant. In the Philippines, street vendors use this familiar sound to attract the attention of potential customers. And in a wide variety of places around the world, men use the kissing sound as a crude but obvious way of "commenting" on the passing of a pretty woman.

Kissing the hand as a form of greeting is regarded by most as a "continental" gesture of worldliness and gentility, although perhaps not to the degree shown here. (See Figure 3.17.) A French book on etiquette says "The man should simply bow low over a woman's hand without actually touching it with his lips, unless it is more than just a polite greeting."

The *fingertip kiss* is also strongly identified with the French (who else?). (Figure 3.18.) It conveys several strains of the basic message "That's good. That's great! That's beautiful!!" It can be seen in all the Romance countries such as France, Italy, Spain, and much of Latin America, and can serve as a laudatory comment on anything from a bottle of wine to a new Ferrari.

The origin of the fingertip kiss probably dates to the custom of ancient Greeks and Romans who, when entering or leaving the temple, threw a kiss to sacred objects such as statues and altars.

From kissing, we move now to other lip and mouth gestures:

Whistling in Europe is a form of jeering. But, not so in the United States where whistling usually conveys approval. And in India it is downright impolite to whistle in public. Americans *hiss*

73

Figure 3.18   The fingertip kiss.

and *boo* to express disapproval. Europeans hiss for silence. In places like Haiti and Spain, they will make noises like "hssssst" and "pssssst" to attract the attention of someone.

Spitting is another sometimes mixed-up signal. For most cultures, spitting in public is considered a rude, crude act. Spitting at someone is an insult, tantamount to a slap in the face.

In other places, spitting has kinder meanings. In the first century A.D., Pliny mentions it as a means of averting witchcraft. The emperor Vespasian, according to Tacitus, cured a blind man by placing his spit on the man's eyes. Both Mark and John also claim in the New Testament that spit applied to the eyes of a blind man restored his sight, adding even further weight to the power of human saliva.

In the People's Republic of China, spitting in public is almost commonplace because there it is regarded as an act of hygiene. It is ridding the body of a waste. The same with blowing the nose, which may be done directly on to the ground, without benefit of a handkerchief. When I once expressed distaste over this custom, my Chinese host said "What's wrong with it? What do *you* do?" When I explained I used a handkerchief for blowing my nose, he countered with "But then you put it back into your pocket. That means you actually carry it around with you all day, doesn't it?"

In 1975, American diplomat Cyrus Vance, soon to become U.S Secretary of State, kept his "cool" when confronted by this business of spitting. He was seated next to China's leader Deng Tso Ping and, as was the custom, between their chairs was a spittoon. Whenever Deng would clear his throat and lean over to expectorate, Vance showed no reaction whatsoever. Observers did note, however, that each time Deng spat, Vance instinctively shifted his foot six inches farther away from the spittoon, then returned it when Deng was finished.

Yawning is a universal sign of tiredness, boredom, or both. But in many countries (France, Belgium, Germany, the United States, Canada, and others) yawning in public is considered impolite . . . and especially so if one does not cover the mouth with the hand. Incidentally, professional speaker H.V. Prochnow defines "protocol" as "learning to yawn with your mouth closed."

Any display of the *open mouth* is considered very rude in Asian countries, particularly Japan and Korea. Have you ever noticed that many Orientals, especially women, cover their mouths when they smile, laugh, or giggle? This is the reason.

In Japan, it is also considered impolite to show your teeth in public, or to sneeze or blow your nose at a business or social gathering.

The *lip point* is a substitute for pointing without using the hand or finger. It is common among Filipinos, native American Indians, Puerto Ricans, and many Latin Americans. The action involves pursing the lips and motioning them in the desired direction.

The *teeth flick*, or "thumbnail flick" as it was called in Chapter 2, involves placing the thumbnail under the upper teeth and then flicking the thumb and fist outward. While it was known and used in Elizabethan England, it is now primarily an Italian gesture meaning anger or a curse or the equivalent of saying "You are nothing!" A variation may be found in Yugoslavia, where the teeth are used to *bite the knuckle* of the forefinger, a gesture that sends the same message.

Picking the teeth with a toothpick in public is, in Italy, a sign that the cuisine was appreciated. In the Orient, it is often done at the dinner table, but always with the other hand discreetly covering the mouth.

The *tongue*, as an instrument of communication, not only helps shape our spoken words but also conveys important unspoken messages. Sticking out the tongue can (1) express derision, as when children stick out their tongues at others, (2) underscore concentration, as when we focus intently on some job at hand, (3) serve as a sexual lure, as when we slowly wet or lick our lips when attracted to another, or (4) indicate greeting, as in some parts of Tibet where people greet one another by sticking out their tongues.

CHIN

In England, the chin is also called the "the pecker," probably because it is involved in "pecking" food. Americans are startled when they hear a Britisher say "Keep your pecker up" (meaning "Keep your chin up").

Whatever you call it, the chin plays just as important a role in our body language as any other part of the body. Some examples follow.

The *chin flick* involves brushing the fingernails of one hand under the chin and then continuing in an outward motion, away from the chin (Figure 3.19). As with many gestures, this has variable meanings, depending on the region:

- In France and Northern Italy, it means "Get lost. You are annoying me."

- In Southern Italy, it is negative but not insulting. It could mean "There is nothing," or "no," or "I cannot."

- In Tunisia, it is insulting.

- In France, it symbolizes a man's beard. Therefore, as an insult it is saying "I throw my masculinity at you."

The *chin stroke* is also associated with a real or imaginary beard, and is therefore a masculine gesture (Figure 3.20). It suggests either (1) contemplation, as if saying "I am thinking," or (2) admiration, as when a man admires a fine painting, a fine car, or a beautiful woman.

Figure 3.19   The chin flick.   **Figure 3.20   The chin stroke.**

The *chin toss* is the same gesture as the *head toss*. The head jerks back and the chin moves upward. It is used as a negation in Southern Italy, Malta, Greece, and Tunisia. In Germany and Scandinavia, it is a beckoning motion. In India, it means "yes."

ARMS

A soccer player, after scoring a goal, thrusts his arms upward and races toward his teammates filled with joy and pride. A boxer, after knocking an opponent senseless, stands over the body, arms raised in obvious glory and triumph. Yet, at the opposite pole is the picture of a defeated soldier raising his arms into the air in surrender, in this case signaling "I carry no weapon."

Curiously, the dramatic gesture of *upraised arms* can signal directly opposite meanings: victory or surrender (Figure 3.21).

Furthermore, politicians raise the arms to incite a crowd, religious followers use them to praise a divine spirit, and an audience of deaf people signal both praise and applause by raising their arms and wiggling their palms.

Sports officials in almost every sporting game have a maze of arm signals to communicate decisions to spectators. The system for signaling with arms and flags, called "semaphore," has been used for centuries aboard ships and on railroad lines.

Some cultures, like the Italians, use the arms freely and enthusiastically. Others, like the Japanese, are more reserved; it is considered impolite in Japanese social or business situations to gesticulate with broad movements of the arms.

Figure 3.21   Victory or surrender.

77

Figure 3.22   There are actually six different ways we fold our arms.

Folded arms are interpreted by some social observers as a form of body language that says "I am taking a defensive posture," or "I disagree with what I am hearing." True or not, anthropologists explain that there are actually *six* different ways we fold our arms—and we each have our own favorite way (Figure 3.22). Try it as an experiment. Take your customary position; then enfold them in a different form; for most it will feel slightly uncomfortable.

Arms akimbo involves standing with the hands on the hips, elbows bowed outward (Figure 3.23). In many cultures, this

Figure 3.23   Arms akimbo.

stance signals aggression, resistance, impatience or even anger. In fact, the word "akimbo" comes from the Old Norse, meaning "bent like a bow," as if to suggest an archer's bow that is bent to launch an arrow.

Tapping the elbow of one arm with the other hand is, in Colombia and a few other Latin areas, a way of saying "He's cheap" or "stingy." In the Netherlands, it could mean "He's unreliable." A variation on this is found in Mexico where, if you lift your left forearm vertically and hit the bottom of the elbow with the palm of the other hand, as if swatting a mosquito, it is considered an insult.

Arms behind the back, hands grasped is, according to some psychologists, a sign of ease and control. It is a way of saying, "I am exposing the front of my body. I have nothing to fear."

An almost universal idiosyncrasy involving the arms occurs when we give directions. If the destination is close, our elbow is bent and the finger is about shoulder high; however, if the destination is far away, we lift the arm higher and stretch it out almost full length. Incidentally, in Japan and China it is more polite when pointing to use the full hand rather than the index finger. Malaysians use the thumb to point, while native American Indians use the chin or "lip pout" rather than pointing with the hand or finger.

Probably the most famous arm gesture of all, though, is the *forearm jerk*, which uses the forearm and hand as an exaggerated phallic symbol (Figure 3.24). No matter the country or language, it is a strong insulting gesture. If you are on the receiving end, beware, be cautious.

Figure 3.24   The most famous arm gesture.

HANDS

Here's a quick test. Ask someone to describe a spiral staircase. Or, ask them to describe an accordion. Nine out of ten people will use their hands, first in a spiral to show how the staircase winds up or down, and then squeezing back and forth across the chest, as when playing an accordion. It's almost automatic, irresistible.

Of all the body parts, the hands are probably used most for sending nonverbal signals. Can there be a more impressive depiction of the hand as a powerful communicator than Michelangelo's painting of the Creator reaching out to touch man's hand?

Desmond Morris observes that we use the hands like a baton to emphasize the rhythm and intent of our words. Furthermore, he proposes that the Italians are the best baton wielders, while the Japanese are the least enthusiastic baton signalers.

Similar motions with our "batons" can send different messages depending on which country we're in. An American student learned this quickly when she went to live in a Japanese home. Her knowledge of Japanese was limited so on her first evening with her host family she kept pointing to herself whenever she wanted to communicate "me." Each time she did this, her hosts would politely point the way to the bathroom. She learned later that in Japan that gesture is interpreted as meaning "I want to go to the bathroom."

Let's look at the baton signals used when a macho male wants to signal the ubiquitous message "Oh! What a pretty girl! If you had a mixed group of men—say an Italian, a Greek, a Brazilian, a Frenchman, and an Arab— you'd see more than a half-dozen different versions of expressing that same thought. Here's how men in those different countries might signal with the hands that they *see a pretty girl.*

- An Italian may use the *cheek screw* as if he is creating a dimple.

- A Greek *strokes his cheek* because in ancient times an egg-shaped face was considered especially beautiful.

- A Brazilian forms two tubes with his hands as though he is *looking through a telescope.*

- A Frenchman *kisses his fingers* which has become known as a special Gallic gesture of praise, whether it be for a pretty woman or a memorable wine.

- An Arab may *stroke his beard.*

- Many South American men will place a *forefinger against their lower eyelid* and pull down slightly, signifying "That's an eyeful."

- An old Italian gesture seen in old American silent movies was the *moustache twist* which suggests a man must preen himself in preparation for his advances toward a girl.

- And finally, in many cultures a man will use both hands to *sweep down an imaginary feminine body* to signal "What a shape!"

Hand-clapping, or applause, is an almost universal way for audiences to express praise and appreciation. But even that common action has its variations:

- Russians and Chinese groups may use applause to *greet* someone. Also, ballet performers in Russia will often applaud back to an appreciative audience, an act that some Westerners misinterpret as egotism.

- Right-handers pound their favored hand down on to the palm of the left land when applauding; left-handers do the opposite.

- In almost all countries, when seated audiences wish to pay special tribute, say, to a head of state or for a superlative performance, they will rise and give a *standing* round of applause.

- In many European countries, particularly in Central and Eastern Europe, audiences frequently *clap in rhythm* as a sign of approval. This is most frequently done at ice skating exhibitions, perhaps because the audience is also keeping time with the musical accompaniment. Visitors to North America, however should know that slow, rhythmic clapping signals *impatience.*

Hand-shaking, as a greeting, is discussed in full detail beginning on page 20.

Hand-holding among males is a custom of special friendship and respect in several Middle Eastern countries. It can also be seen in places like Korea, parts of China, and Indochina. In those parts of the world, it should not be misconstrued as an indication of homosexuality. In parts of North America, however, particularly in cities with large gay populations like San Francisco or New York, it is common to see two gay men proudly exhibiting their affection via this gesture.

The *right hand* has special significance in many societies. For example, in courtrooms witnesses are asked to raise their right hand to swear oaths of truthfulness. Also, the idiom "a left-handed compliment" means an insincere or twisted compliment, and the French word for left, *gauche,* in English means "crude" or "awkward." As a result, in certain countries in the Middle East and the Orient it is best to present business cards or gifts, or to pass dishes of food, using only the right hand.

The *left hand* is considered the "unclean" hand in much of the Middle East because it is customarily reserved for bodily hygiene. There, lavatories are often not equipped with either a toilet bowl or toilet tissue. Bathrooms frequently consist of just a hole in the floor, perhaps with indentations on either side for the feet, plus a nearby water faucet. There may also be a small pitcher in which to pour the water on to the hands. Thus, one cleans oneself with the left hand and the water.

This custom is especially important to remember because, as a consequence, at communal dinners where food is often touched with the hands, the left hand should *never* be used for eating. Furthermore, as a form of punishment in that part of the world, criminals have their right hands amputated. That person is forced to live with only one hand, the "unclean" hand, and will probably be shunned by society as a result.

Hand-waves, used for greetings or beckoning or farewells, are described in detail in Chapter 2, beginning on page 28. There you will find more information on the following common hand gestures used for greeting or beckoning another person:

- The *namaste,* or *wai,* where the hands form a praying position, is the customary greeting in places like India and Thailand.

- The *salaam,* a sweeping motion with the hand, going from heart to head and outward, and is still used in parts of the Middle East.

As for waving "hello" or "good-bye," or when trying to gain someone's attention, there are actually *three different* signals:

- The *hand-waggle,* with the whole hand waggling back and forth, left to right, is the custom in North America.

- The *hand-bob,* with the hand bobbing up and down at the wrist, as if patting some object, is more common in Europe.

- The *palm upward, finger-scratching* inward motion is peculiar to Italy.

When *beckoning* someone, in the United States, the hand may be raised and the *index finger curled* back and forth. However, in places like Indonesia, Hong Kong, Australia and others this is used only for calling animals so it would be impolite to direct at any human.

The *hand push* is peculiar to Greece, and is considered an insulting gesture. It originates from ancient times when dirt or even feces were rubbed in the face of captured enemies.

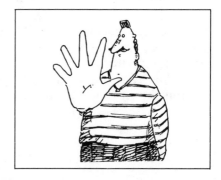

More *insulting hand gestures* are illustrated and described in Chapter 2 (see pages 33–42). Here is a brief review of the main ones:

- *The finger* is usually accompanied by a jerking upward motion of the hand. It is a phallic symbol and says, "Up yours!"

- The *ear-waggle* uses the hands at either side of the head to imitate a donkey, which is considered slow and stupid.

- *Thumbing the nose* involves the thumb and hand extending from the nose and is an age-old mocking gesture used by many cultures.

- The *thumbnail flick* or *thumb bite* is performed by making a fist with the hand and pretending to bite the tip of the thumb or thumbnail. It is synonymous with the word "insult."

- *Shaking the fist* is an almost universal gesture signaling anger, resentment, and opposition.

- *Slapping a fist* upward into the palm of the other hand is, in such widely separated places like France and Chile, a demonstrative way of saying "Up yours!"

Another insulting gesture among males (also considered vulgar) is the *crotch grab*. As the name implies, it simply involves grabbing the genitals with one hand, usually rather vigorously. The meaning is strongly sexual and insulting. In Argentina, the same message is sent by a man who uses both hands to slap down and grab his own inner thighs.

The *hand purse* is as Italian as pizza, pasta, and the Tower of Pisa (Figure 3.25). Among Italians, it is used for punctuating and emphasizing speech. It also conveys different emotions. For example, if the fingers are gripped tightly and the hand jerked abruptly it conveys strength or anger. If the fingers are gripped lightly and the motion is gentle, it might signal preciseness or delicacy. Indeed, there are so many nuances to this distinctly Italian gesture that it could warrant a special guidebook of its own. Incidentally, it may be seen in a few other European countries, but Italy is truly its home territory.

The *fig* is one of the more confusing hand gestures because in some countries it is an insult, in others it sends sexual signals,

Figure 3.25   The hand purse.

and in still other parts of the world it is a signal for "good luck." (Figure 3.26.)

Desmond Morris claims that the *fig*—a clenched fist with the thumb coming through between the knuckle of the index and middle fingers—was popular in ancient Rome where it represented a "penis inserted through labia." Through the ages, this was somehow twisted around to also convey "good luck." Here are three regions where those separate interpretations prevail:

- In Brazil, replicas of this gesture have become a popular charm for necklaces or bracelets because it is believed this gesture wards off evil. There it is called the *figa*, incidentally, and means "good luck."

- In Greece and Turkey, it is considered an insulting gesture, as if displaying the symbolic phallus in a taunting fashion.

- In Tunisia and Holland, it has strong sexual connotations.

As if to add even further confusion, it has yet a fourth meaning in Yugoslavia. There it is used to signal "nothing," as when a mother might say to a child, "No, you cannot have any ice cream."

As for historical documentation for this gesture, Dante, in his *Inferno* (XXV, 1–3) wrote: "When he had finished, the thief—to his disgrace—raised his arms with both fists making figs, and cried, 'Here God. I throw them in your face!'"

The *"hang loose"* gesture with thumb and little finger extended is popular in Hawaii and is a way of saying "Stay cool," or

Figure 3.26   The fig.

Figure 3.27   "Hang loose."

"Relax." (Figure 3.27.) In Mexico, when this gesture is done vertically in front of the body (knuckles pointing outward) it means
"Would you like a drink?" In this case, the hand and fingers represent a handle to a mug. And in Japan, this positioning of the
fingers signals the number "six," since the thumb represents "five"
and the little finger adds one more digit to equal "six."

A variation on the "hang loose" gesture is the American Sign
Language shorthand version of the message *"I love you."* (Figure
3.28.) You may see rock stars, politicians, clergy, and others flashing this signal to their audiences. Also, G.I.s in "Operation Desert
Storm" were seen flashing this gesture at TV cameras.

The *"high five"* gesture developed from the sports world.
When congratulating one another, teammates originally would
shake hands; that handshake later evolved into a more enthusiastic

Figure 3.28   American Sign Language shorthand for "I love you."

Figure 3.29   The high five.

slap of the palms (one player holds the palm upward, the other player slaps down on it). In recent years, this same slapping motion moved upward into the air (Figure 3.29). It is seen largely in the United States, but is moving quickly through the international sporting world. A new variation among American baseball players is to bump elbows of teammates, and American football players have taken to bumping their helmets against one another.

Also from the sports world, is the "time out" gesture. The hands form the letter "T," and it is commonly seen in American football and basketball (Figure 3.30).

Figure 3.30   Time out.

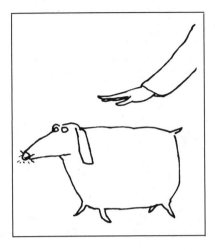

Using the *hands to measure lengths or heights* would seem a simple and uncomplicated process. But in some Latin American countries it can be a tricky business, particularly in Colombia. As for *heights,* there are two different ways, depending on if one is referring to a human or to an animal. To designate the height of an *animal,* a Colombian puts the palm downward, but to show the height of a *person,* the *edge* of the palm points downward.

Also in Colombia, one does *not* designate *lengths* by extending the forefingers of each hand as is the custom in most parts of the world. In Colombia, this is considered a rude gesture. Instead, to demonstrate the length of an object, a person extends the hand and forearm (palm held vertically) and then shows the desired length with the vertical palm of the other hand.

Suicide gestures are different, depending on the country:

- In the United States, a person points a forefinger to the temple, thumb pointing upward, to resemble a pistol.

- In Japan, a stabbing motion to the stomach conveys the same message, as if committing *hari kari*.

- In New Guinea, putting one hand to the throat in a choking motion is the signal for suicide.

However, in North America the choking gesture can also have two other meanings:

- In American sporting circles, it means "I choked," meaning "I tensed up" or "I froze up" and therefore performed badly.

- A far more serious interpretation is that the person is actually choking. When a person lodges a piece of food in the throat, it is impossible to cough, breathe or talk. Bystanders often misinterpret the frantic actions of that person as a heart attack or some other malady and may apply the wrong type of first aid. As a result, the American Red Cross is trying to train people to use this choking gesture to signal "I am choking! Please help me by applying the correct aid to help dislodge food!"

Using the hand to toast others goes back to Roman times and seems a simple matter, but it can have important social nuances. For example, it is important to have good eye contact with the guest of honor or the chief host while toasting. In the Orient, a toast is often accompanied by the word *kam-pie*, which means "bottoms up" and it may even be proper protocol to actually turn your glass upside down to demonstrate that you have, indeed, emptied the glass. Also, among more traditional Swedes, the

proper toasting motion "begins from the seventh button
down on the waistcoat up-
ward to the eyes, followed by
a nod of the head, a drink,
good and direct eye contact,
and then lower the glass down
to the seventh button once
again."

Another bit of toasting
lore is found in England
where, even today, some pewter mugs are fitted with glass bottoms. The reason for this is that centuries ago unsuspecting sailors
were shanghaied into military service when a "recruiter" would
secretly slip a coin into a mug of ale. Then, as the sailor emptied
the mug, the coin would fall to his lips. At that time in England,
the act of kissing the coin of the Crown was considered a form of
pledging service and loyalty. As the victim drank, the coin would
touch his lips thereby unwittingly "enlisting" him into naval service. As a precaution, mugs were fitted with glass bottoms so the
drinker could see what lay on the bottom and thereby avoid this
unwanted gesture of fealty.

Knocking on wood can be traced back to the days before
Christ. It has come to signify a jumble of meanings: showing
reverence for the Christian (wooden) cross, knocking on
(wooden) church doors for sanctuary, a form of tree worship, or
even knocking on Heaven's door. The English say "touch wood"
while Americans use "knock on wood," all to bring good luck.
The Finns believe it is important to knock on bare wood, and
therefore may be seen knocking *under* a table rather than on top.

The *hand pat* to the back of the hand in the Netherlands is
a signal denoting that someone else is gay. It is done by brushing
the fingers of one hand across or on top of the back of the other
hand (Figure 3.31).

Figure 3.31   The hand pat.

Figure 3.32   The hand sweep.

The *hand sweep* may be seen in Latin America and means that "someone is stealing" or "getting away with something." In Peru, it means "money" or "pay me." It is done by making a sweeping or grabbing motion with the hand toward the body, as though sweeping chips off a table (Figure 3.32).

The *flat hand flick* is an almost universal gesture meaning "go away" or "get lost." It is done by holding the palm downward and flicking the fingers away from the body (Figure 3.33). According to an article in the Jerusalem Post, to an Israeli this gesture says "Enough already," yet to an Ethiopian it means "I love you."

A *hand saw* across the forehead expresses the message "I've had it up to here," or "I'm in deep, over my head." The hand cuts across the top of the head, as if saying "I'm in deep water up to here." (Figure 3.34.)

The *hand wag* is performed by pointing the hand outward, palm down, fingers spread, and then waggling the whole hand up

Figure 3.33   The flat hand flick.

Figure 3.34   The hand saw.

and down (i.e., thumb up, thumb down, thumb up again, and so on). (Figure 3.35.) In the United States and Europe, it is often done in response to "How are you?" or "How does it go?" and means "Just so-so." "Not good. Not bad." In Holland and other countries, it can also be used to signal "Oh, it's very tricky."

The *hitch-hiking* gesture is predominantly a North American gesture, used on highways to signal "I need a ride." It is done by making a fist, thumb up and then making a sweeping motion, pointing the thumb in the direction the person wishes to go. Americans should be extra cautious about exporting this gesture, however. Author James C. Simmons reports that in 1972, three

Figure 3.35   The hand wag.

Figure 3.36   The hand flap.

young American college men were sexually assaulted while hitch-hiking across Turkey from Istanbul to Ankara. In many parts of that country, he writes, this is a symbol used as an invitation for a homosexual encounter. In places like Sardinia, Greece, and parts of West Africa, it is generally an insulting gesture, meaning "Get stuffed."

The *hand flap* may be seen in South Africa. It is performed by stiffening the four fingers and flapping them down against the thumb, as is imitating the bill of a duck (Figure 3.36). I once drove from Johannesburg to Pretoria and spotted people along the side of the road making this gesture at me. I assumed it was some sort of greeting, so I "flapped" back at them. When I arrived in Pretoria, I got out of the car and then noticed my left turn signal had been blinking. It wasn't until that moment that I realized those helpful South Africans were signaling to me that my left turn signal was flashing on and off. And what had I done? I had signaled back to them, saying, in effect "So is yours!"

Cupped hands appear to be the universal signal for begging. In South Africa, a new arrival may observe porters at airports holding out their hands in this fashion. They are saying "The gift you may give me for carrying your bags will mean so much, I must hold it in two hands."

Hand salute is, in many countries, the military gesture for conveying respect to a higher ranking officer. Historians believe that the salute probably originates from medieval days when knights in armour raised their visors to one another as a signal that they meant no harm. Yet, in Italy, a salute to the forehead also means "You're *pazzo* (crazy)."

Keeping ones *hands in ones pockets* when conversing in either social and business situations is considered an impolite posture in such diverse locales as Belgium, Indonesia, France, Finland, Japan, and Sweden.

Hands on hips in Indonesia and many Latin American countries may well be interpreted as a gesture of defiance or challenge.

Some Universal Hand Gestures

- Pressing the palms together and resting the head on the back of the hand while closing the eyes as if sleeping is generally understood as saying "I am tired."

- Patting the stomach with the hands usually means "I am full."

- Taking the hand and making a circular motion over the stomach signals "I am hungry."

- Using the hand to mimic the act of drinking is a way of gesturing the message "I am thirsty."

- Rubbing the hands together can mean (1) "I am cold," (2) "Oh, that's nice," (3) "It's cozy" or (4) a sign of eager anticipation.

Folded hands, with fingers intertwined is a gesture seen around the world. But there is one peculiarity worth noting: each of us has a favorite thumb that we consistently place on top. Try it. Fold your hands in your customary fashion. Now switch the position of the thumbs. It usually feels slightly uncomfortable (Figure 3.37).

Crossing the heart with the hand is a Christian rite harkening back to the crucifix. Just as many people "cross the fingers" as a pledge of faith or good luck, Christians make this sign over the

Figure 3.37   Are you right-thumbed or left?

upper body. According to Tad Tuleja, author of *Curious Customs* (Stonesong Press, 1987), in early times it was done with thumb and forefinger at the forehead. By the fourth century, the heart was also crossed. By the tenth century, full upper-body crossing was the custom. "From the thirteenth century on," Tuleja writes, "Eastern-rite Catholics use the thumb and first two fingers (symbolizing the Trinity) and touch the right shoulder first. Roman-rite followers use the full five digits (supposedly representing Christ's five wounds) and touch the left shoulder first."

Where do you place your hands while eating? On top of or beneath the table? American mothers teach their children to place the left hand in the lap; many European mothers teach just the opposite, that both hands should remain above or on the table. The reasons for keeping both hands visible apparently date back to the sixteenth century. One explanation is that this demonstrated that no weapons were being concealed below the table. Another is that both hands on the table assured that there was no sexual hanky-panky going on among tablemates.

The *fist slap* in several countries (France, Italy, and Chile, to name just three) can signify a very strong, rude message saying "Up yours!" It can be done in two ways: (1) by holding the palm of one hand downward and smacking the fist of the other hand up and into that palm, (2) the fist can be held stationery and the palm of the other hand can slap down on top. Visitors to the United States should note that Americans and others may do this gesture in casual idleness, with no special significance or message. By the same token, Americans visiting the locales noted above should avoid any such casual, idle swinging and slapping of the hands (Figure 3.38).

Fist pounding is generally understood to signal anger and determination. It can be done with either hand onto a hard surface, or into the palm of the other hand. One graphic example of fist pounding was that of Soviet Premier Nikita Krushchev who pounded first his fist and then his shoe on his desk at the United Nations back in the late 1950s.

Figure 3.38   The fist slap.

Two fists, with thumbs tucked inside and then gently thrust in a downward motion, is a Germanic way of saying "Good luck!" (Figure 3.39.) While others may cross their fingers as a message and wish for "Good luck," Germans will use this distinctive "two fists" gesture instead.

Rapping the knuckles on wood is, according to Morris, akin to "touching the sacred oak to placate the god Thor." It is done after making a wish or boast. Swedes may rap underneath a table in order to assure touching bare wood. In Germany, however, this gesture is also used for two rather delightful welcoming messages. For example, students at universities will greet their professors at the beginning of a class by rapping knuckles on desks as a signal of greeting and respect. Also, when dining at a large communal table, as people arrive or leave the table, they may be seen and heard to rap the table lightly. It is a form of greeting or

Figure 3.39   Good luck!

Figure 3.40 The bird flap.

farewell and a substitute for the inconvenience of rising and walking around the table to shake hands.

The *bird flap* gesture involves placing the palm of one hand over the back of the other, with thumbs extended, and wiggling the thumbs to imitate a flying bird (Figure 3.40). In Colombia, this is a sign to denote a homosexual.

The *copulation gesture* is known in many countries and is both descriptive and graphic. The forefinger of one hand is inserted into a ring formed by the thumb and forefinger of the other hand to represent the act of copulation (Figure 3.41).

Now, here's a closing question. Have you ever considered how an audience of deaf people applaud? No, they don't pound their hands together to create an audible wave of sound. Rather, they have conceived a beautiful *sight* to replace the sound of applause. They raise their hands to either side of the head and waggle them furiously creating what assuredly is a heart-warming picture of waves and waves of fingers in motion signaling this very special form of appreciation (Figure 3.42).

Figure 3.41 Nearly universal—and none-too-subtle.

Figure 3.42   How a deaf person applauds.

FINGERS

Anyone who has cut or sprained a finger knows how our lives can become instantly more cumbersome. We fumble over buttons, miss keys on typewriters, misdial telephones, and have trouble gripping objects. It's so vexing our whole temperament is affected. And without our fingers our daily communication would be severely warped—both our spoken and our non-verbal communication.

For example, many figures of speech rely heavily on the fingers: We speak of a finger of land; we finger cloth or a musical instrument; a snitch "fingers" a miscreant; we "wrap someone around our finger"; we burn our fingers; we put them in pies; they are indispensable for counting; our drinkers ask for "a couple fingers of whiskey"; and, finally, our fingers provide one-fifth of our senses, our sense of touch.

We use the fingers extensively in our nonverbal communication. Here are some examples.

"The finger," as we call it, is notorious worldwide. "The finger wave," the "bird," the "bone," the "one-finger salute," the "impudent finger," and the "expressway digit" are just a few of its English synonyms. Who knows how many novel synonyms exist in dozens of other languages (Figure 3.43).

As we learned in Chapter 2 (see page 34), "The finger" has been used as an insult for over 2,000 years. Middle Easterners modify it by pointing it downward, and just about all historians agree it is considered rude and obscene because of its phallic symbolism.

Figure 3.43   The one-finger salute.

The "O.K." signal was also discussed in detail in Chapter 2. (see page 47). Here, the thumb and forefinger form a simple circle . . . but then the confusion begins:

- In most societies, it is recognized as an American-born gesture for "Everything is fine," or "Everything if O.K." Desmond Morris supposes that it originates from putting the thumb and forefinger together as if holding something very small, thus suggesting "precision" or "just right."

- In France it means "zero" or "worthless," and in Japan it is the signal for "money."

- And in a host of other countries—Brazil being the best known—it is considered very rude because it is seen to represent the female genitalia. Ancient vases, some 2,000 years old, depict males using this signal as an insult. And an insult it is likely to be in the following countries: Malta, Sardinia, Greece, Brazil, Tunisia, Italy, Turkey, the Soviet Union, and Paraguay.

Our *thumb* is a very special digit because of its singular versatility. It not only sets humans apart in the animal world because it affords us special grasping abilities, but it also expressively communicates so many varied messages. Here are some examples:

- We learned in Chapter 2 all about the *"thumbs up"* gesture (see page 49), and how it ranges from meaning everything from "Right on!" to something very rude, (i.e., in Australia, "Up yours, mate!") (Figure 3.44).

- The thumb is also the dominant feature when *hitch-hiking*. But, as a few Western hitch-hikers have learned, in some countries (Nigeria being one), the upright thumb, whether in motion or not, is considered an insult.

- In Germany, the upright thumb is a signal for the *number* "one." But in Japan, that identical upright thumb signifies the number "five."

- Both the phrase and the gesture *"thumbs down"* mean that something is bad or rejected, and that interpretation reaches as far back as Roman times. It is seen on ancient Roman frescos. But, interestingly, there are no known depictions of the "thumbs up" gesture as meaning "O.K." or "Good" or "He shall live," as we have been led to believe, probably by Hollywood movies.

- When Germans wish to signal "Good Luck," they *tuck the thumb into the fist*. They may even do it with both fists, and then make a slight up-and-down or pounding motion.

- In Malaysia, when *pointing*, the thumb is favored over the forefinger or other fingers.

Figure 3.44 "Up yours, mate!"

- In Spain, displaying an upward thumb is the *symbol for support* of the Basque separatist movement, and therefore it becomes a political statement that can actually incite strong discord.

- In summary, a thumb sitting upright on a clenched fist is considered *a rude signal* in the following countries: Australia (especially when jerked upward slightly), Sardinia, Iran, Ghana and the Soviet Union.

When and where the thumb is used in conjunction with the other fingers it increases the message-sending possibilities many-fold. Here are some examples:

- *Rubbing the thumb and forefinger together* sends several different signals. The most common one is "money." Rubbing the thumb and forefinger back and forth in this manner apparently mimics the gesture of thumbing folding money. It also mimics the action of feeling a fabric, or accompanies the question "What does it feel like?"

- *Squeeze the thumb and forefinger tightly together* and many people in the Mediterranean region will consider it vulgar because it supposedly depicts the vagina. Yet in France, this gesture may be used to send the visual signal that something is "Perfect," as in the statement "It is *this* close . . so close that it is almost perfect" (Figure 3.45).

Figure 3.45 A Mediterranean vulgarity that is almost perfect in France.

Pointing with the index finger is common in North America and Europe, but it is considered impolite in Japan and China where they favor using the whole open hand. Malaysians prefer pointing with the thumb rather than the forefinger. Incidentally, among native American Indians it is considered impolite to point with the fingers. Instead, they use pointed lips or their chins.

Authors Lennie Copeland and Lewis Griggs once asked an Englishman, "If it is impolite to point out someone, how do you do it without pointing?" Their companion dropped a shoulder, raised his eyebrows and jerked his head to the side, as though tossing it in the direction he meant to point. The authors said, "Clear as day, he pointed without pointing."

Extending the forefinger and little finger, like horns, while keeping the other fingers in a fist, was discussed in detail in Chapter 2 (see page 53). At the University of Texas, this represents the horns of a longhorn steer, the school symbol. Yet this same "horn" gesture in Italy signals that someone is being cuckolded. In some African countries, it is seen as casting a spell or a curse, and in Brazil it means "good luck."

The *"V for victory"* signal (index and middle fingers forming a "V" shape) is also discussed in Chapter 2 (see page 51). There you will learn its probable origins plus how this gesture and a 180-degree twist of the wrist can get you into a heap of trouble.

Rubbing the forefinger of one hand over the forefinger of the other hand is used in North America and recognized in parts of Europe to issue the reproof "Shame on you."

Waggling the forefinger back and forth is a fairly common and widespread gesture used to chastise someone, as if saying "No, no. Don't do that." The Japanese, however, expand on that and waggle the whole hand, palm outward, and in their case they are probably signaling "No, no. I am not worthy."

Crossing the fingers in North America and many parts of Europe is an expression of "Good Luck" and is probably derived from the cross of Christ. However, it is also done, usually in jest, when telling a "white lie," as if making the sign of the cross defends and protects one from committing a sin. In Paraguay, crossed fingers can be considered offensive (Figure 3.46).

Tapping the two forefingers together and side-by-side is a gesture that may be seen in places like Egypt. There it signifies "Would you like to go to bed with me?" (Figure 3.47).

Snapping the fingers may be a way of either getting someone's attention, or perhaps keeping time to music. But, snapping the fingers of *both* hands at the same time can have vulgar meanings in places like France and some Latin countries.

Figure 3.46   Don't cross in Paraguay.

There are numerous and diverse gestures involving the fingers in connection with the head and face. These are described in earlier parts of this chapter, but here is a digest:

- *Tapping the temple with the forefinger* can either mean "Intelligence" or "He (or she) is crazy."

- However, tapping the *center of the forehead* with the forefinger is, in The Netherlands, a way of silently saying "He's crazy."

Figure 3.47   An Egyptian proposition.

- Taking the forefinger and pretending to screw it into the *temple or the cheek* is another way of sending messages. Italian men twist the forefinger into the *cheek* when they see a pretty girl. German auto drivers may be seen twisting the forefinger into the *temple* when some other driver has behaved badly; in fact, so strong a gesture is this in Germany that one can reputedly be arrested for doing it.

- *Kissing the fingertips* of the first three fingers is identified as a popular French gesture and signals a silent, graphic way of saying *"magnifique!"*

- Lifting the hand up, palm out, and extending the (1) thumb, (2) forefinger, and (3) little finger is shorthand in American Sign Language for the message *"I love you!"*

As a closing note to this segment on finger gestures, I once interviewed two retired Central Intelligence Agency operatives at a dinner party in Washington, DC, asking if they knew of any unusual, unique gestures from around the world. Here is one story they related to me:

> Sikhs are part of a Hindu religious sect, distinguished by their colorful turbans and full beards. Today in New York City, many of them have taken up occupations as taxi drivers. If you should happen to employ a taxi driven by a Sikh, be watchful for one particular gesture. If traffic is heavy and tempers are fraying, watch to see if the Sikh *taps the face of his wristwatch* with his forefinger. If so, it has a special, almost ominous meaning to all those around. That simple gesture is a Sikh way of saying "It's twelve o'clock, and all Sikhs go mad at noon." In effect, it says ". . . watch your step. Check the time. It may be close to noon. That's when I go mad!"

LEGS AND FEET

"Putting your foot in your mouth" is just one of many ways to verbally offend someone using odd parts of the body. Here are other ways to offend when using the legs or feet.

Showing the sole of your shoe is a physical action that sends a rude message in many parts of the Middle East and Far East.

In one case, it even resulted in a murder (see page 11, Chapter 1). Specific places where this is offensive are: Saudi Arabia, Egypt, Singapore, or Thailand. Since the sole of the shoe is obviously the lowest and dirtiest part of the body, it's not difficult to accept that in some cultures it is a mighty effective way to flash an insult.

In some of the countries listed above, it is also the custom to sit on cushions on the floor. As a result, some Westerners complain that "You have to be a contortionist to sit crosslegged on the floor and still not innocently point your sole at another person." Nonetheless, be careful. Watch how others do it. Keep your soles hidden by sitting on them or by tucking them underneath your knees.

In Thailand, *don't point with your toes.* There, the head is considered almost sacred and the foot is considered lowly and inferior. While it seems unreasonable that any of us might be in a situation where we would—or even could—point our toes at someone's head, in Thailand this would be the most grievous insult possible. The same applies for pointing your toes at a religious object.

Another taboo would be *putting up your feet on a desk* or any other piece of furniture. This taboo applies in many countries, including Thailand, Japan, and France. Once again, the symbolism here is that you are pointing the lowest part of your body at someone; or, in a milder form, you are showing disrespect by such an exhibit of casual informality.

Do you *cross your legs* when seated? Many people do. In fact, there are four distinct styles of sitting cross-legged. They are:

1. Legs crossed at ankles,

2. Legs crossed at knees,

3. One ankle resting on the knee of the other leg, and

4. Legs crossed at the knees and foot entwined around that same leg.

In some places, however, sitting crosslegged sends the wrong signals. In Thailand, it is considered so improper that a well-known Thai woman reformer and journalist was once physically removed from Parliament when she refused to uncross her legs.

In England (as noted in Chapter 1), what might be known as the "Royal Cross" consists of crossing the legs at the ankles, but not at the knees. Observe news photographs of English royalty, especially Queen Elizabeth II, and you'll see that Victorian primness prevails. She is almost always pictured with legs crossed at the ankles and never at the knees. Princess Diana, however, is often pictured with her legs crossed at the knees, proving that even royal conventions change.

Style 1

Style 2

Style 3

Style 4

In America, crossing the legs at the knee was at one time considered a somewhat effeminate posture, although it is very common now among both men and women. It is perhaps even more common among men in Europe. A second, more masculine crosslegged pose for American men is to rest the ankle of one leg on top of the knee of the other leg. Rarely would a woman be seen in such a position, unless she is wearing slacks.

A very feminine crosslegged pose occurs when a woman not only crosses the legs at the knees, but manages to also curl the upper foot around the calf of the lower leg in a virtual "figure eight." Men rarely, if ever, do it . . . maybe because they can't!

Whichever of these you prefer, be observant in the country you are visiting and consider following suit. In Japan, for instance, a solid and balanced sitting posture is the prevailing custom, so that it is probably best to keep both feet planted squarely on the floor. And in the Middle East and parts of Southeast Asia, resting the ankle over the other knee risks pointing the sole of your shoe at another person which, as we have already said, is considered a rude gesture in those regions.

In Japan it is often the custom to *remove one's shoes* before entering private homes, restaurants, inns, and tea and geisha houses. This practice is hard to miss, since you will not only see others removing their shoes, but you'll also quickly spot a row of shoes at the entrances—neatly arranged with toes pointing out-ward, away from the door. This is also the custom in Moslem countries. There, shoes are removed before entering some homes and always before entering mosques.

Even the *way we stand* can send messages. For example, standing with feet apart can be interpreted as being both aggres-sive and very masculine. A feminine posture, on the other hand, would have feet closer together and one toe pointed inward. Wide stances are regarded as masculine the world over, and nar-row stances are considered feminine; women fashion models adopt narrow stances, while a husky male football player stands with feet planted wide.

Anyone who has served in the military is trained to stand with *heels together,* toes pointed out at a slight angle. As a result, this has become a posture that exhibits respect and attention in the presence of superiors. However, *clicking the heels* is no longer practiced except, perhaps, in parody of the Prussian signal for "At your service," where it seems to have originated.

FULL BODY

The feminine *curtsy* and the religious *genuflection* are probably two of the best known gestures involving the full body. Moslems *kneel* at prayer and prostrate themselves with arms forward.

The male counterpart of the curtsy is the *bow,* but with the exception of Japan neither is commonplace or observed, except in the presence of true royalty. Even then, if anyone other than a British citizen should meet the Queen, proper decorum is for women to dip slightly and for men to bow the head downward slightly at the neck.

There are very few other full–body gestures that are consid-ered "acquired" gestures and that vary from country to country. One fascinating, apparently instinctive full–body gesture is what Desmond Morris and other anthropologists have called "postural echo," something found in most societies. This refers to how friends who are conversing will often adopt similar body postures. This is usually not deliberate, scientists point out, but it happens frequently. If one person leans on a table with the elbows and tilts his or her head, the other person is likely to do the same.

Walking can reflect many characteristics of a culture. For example, Latin men who are friends may walk with arms linked. In Chapter 2 the segment on "Touching" (see page 42) describes cultures where men actually walk hand-in-hand.

In the Far East, notably in Japan and Korea, women customarily walk a pace or two behind male companions. Oriental women often regard Western women as bold and aggressive, largely because Western women appear to walk with a longer gait and a more upright posture.

4

The Ultimate
Gesture

I f you are bewildered by the seemingly infinite number of gestures used around the world, and the nuances, shades of differences and contradictions that separate them, perhaps this is the best point at which to introduce the "ultimate gesture." I call it that because it carries certain welcome characteristics unlike any other single gesture.

- First, this "ultimate gesture" is known everywhere—and I stress "everywhere"—in the world. It is absolutely universal.

- Second, it is rarely, if ever, misunderstood. Primitive tribes and world leaders alike know and use this gesture. The tribesmen— like you, no doubt—recognize it in others and use it themselves.

- Third, scientists believe this particular gesture actually releases chemicals called endorphins into the system that create a feeling of mild euphoria.

- Fourth, as you travel around the world this gesture may help you slip out of the pricklyist of difficult situations.

What is this singular signal, this miracle mien, this giant of all gestures?
It is, quite simply, the smile.
Use if freely. Use it often.

5

THE INNOCENT ABROAD'S SHORTLIST

You are planning a trip overseas, or hosting an international visitor. When it comes to communications via gestures and body language, how can you separate *right* from *rude,* and *rude* from *crude?*

Here is a shortlist of the 20 gestures and body language most commonly used by North Americans. To avoid misunderstandings, the single best piece of advice is to be observant and sensitive to what's going on around you. And don't be afraid to ask.

1. SHAKING HANDS

Here: When greeting one another, North Americans shake hands, and from an early age they are taught to do so with a firm, solid grip.

There: While hand-clasping as a greeting has generally been adopted around the world, the Japanese prefer to greet one another by bowing (but will quickly cater to Westerners by shaking hands). Southeast Asians press their own palms together in a praying motion. And when Middle Easterners and many Orientals shake hands, they favor a *gentle* grip. That is because in their cultures a firm grip suggests aggressiveness.

2. EYE CONTACT

Here: When greeting and conversing with others, North American children are taught to look others directly in the eyes. To do otherwise is often regarded as a sign of shyness, or lack of warmth or—even worse—as weakness.

There: Japanese and Korean parents train their children to do just the opposite: *Avert* the eyes and *avoid* direct eye contact. Direct eye contact is, to them, considered intimidating or may indicate sexual overtones.

3. WAVING

Here: Whether North Americans are signaling "Hello" or "Goodbye", or simply trying to get the attention of some distant person, they raise the arm and waggle the open hand back and forth.

There: Throughout much of Europe this action signals "No!" When bidding a greeting or farewell, Europeans customarily raise the arm and *bob the hand up and down at the wrist,* similar to the wrist action when dribbling a basketball. And Italians may use an entirely different version: palm *up,* fingers curling inward, back and forth.

4. BECKONING

Here: North Americans will often summon another person by waving (to get their attention) and then turning the hand to make hand scoops inward. Another beckoning motion Americans might use is to raise the index finger (palm toward one's face) and make a *curling motion* with that finger.

There: Both of these beckoning gestures may be misunderstood in other parts of the world. Throughout Europe the gesture that means "Come here" is done by raising the arm, *palm facing down,* and then make a scratching motion with the fingers. As for the curling of the index finger, in places like Australia and Indonesia that is used only for beckoning *animals* and never for humans.

5. "V" FOR VICTORY

Here: Display the index and middle fingers in the shape of a "V" and virtually all over the world it is understood to mean "victory" or "peace."

There: Be careful, however, in England. There, when this same gesture is done with *the palm facing inward toward the face* it is tantamount to signaling "Up yours!"

6. THE "O.K." GESTURE

Here: North Americans flash this gesture frequently and enthusiastically: It's done by forming a circle with thumb and forefinger with the other three fingers splayed upward.

There: However, take care in France where this means "zero" or "worthless," or in Japan where it can mean "money," as if making the shape of a coin. In places like Brazil, the U.S.S.R., and Germany it is the signal for a very private bodily orifice. So in those countries, the American signal for "O.K." is definitely not.

7. THUMBS UP

Here: North Americans and many other cultures flash this nearly ubiquitous gesture when they want to silently say "Good job!", "O.K.!" or "Great!" or a dozen other expressions, all of which demonstrate support and approval.

There: In certain locales, however, it can carry completely different meanings. In Australia, if the thumb is pumped up-and-down it is the equivalent of saying "Up Yours!" Also, where North Americans may use the upright thumb when hitch-hiking, in countries like Nigeria it is considered a rude gesture and should be avoided. In Japan and Germany the upraised thumb is also used when counting: in Japan it signifies "five," but in Germany it is the signal for "one."

8. "HOOK 'EM HORNS"

Here: Most Texans will recognize this gesture (fist raised with index finger and little finger extended) as a University of Texas rallying call because it mimics the horns of the school's symbol and mascot, the famous Texas Longhorn steer.

There: But, in Italy this same gesture means someone is being cuckolded. In Africa, it can mean the levying of a curse. And in Brazil and Venezuela, the same gesture is considered a good luck sign to ward off evil.

9. SPACE RELATIONSHIPS

Here: In normal social situations, North Americans generally stand about 30-inches apart from one another. That's considered the personal "comfort zone" and is equal to about an arm's length.

There: Orientals, however, usually stand *farther* apart. In contrast, Latins and Middle Easterners stand *much closer*— sometimes even toe-to-toe, or side-to-side brushing elbows. As a result, North Americans need to steel themselves for such close encounters because to move away sends an unfriendly message.

10. TOUCHING

Here: North Americans are not touch-oriented. With good friends, they may occasionally touch a forearm or elbow, and with *very* good friends they may go so far as placing an arm around a shoulder. But *hugging* is almost never done among casual acquaintances.

There: While Orientals join Americans in shunning such bodily contact, Latins seem to dote on it with hearty embraces and warm pats to the back. In the Middle East, two Arab male friends may even be seen walking down the street hand-in-hand and all it signifies is friendship.

11. KISSING

Here: Among North Americans, kissing is usually reserved for sweethearts, one's mother, and among close female relatives, but rarely between two men.

There: Among Latins, Southern Europeans, and Russians, both male and female acquaintances will commonly greet one another with busses to the cheeks. These are more likely a feigned kiss to one cheek, sometimes both cheeks, and maybe even a "triple play": one cheek, the other cheek, and then back to the first cheek again. Incidentally, the Continental practice of kissing a lady's hand has almost disappeared—except among a few pockets of gallants in Italy and other Romance language cultures.

12. TOASTING

Here: North Americans will occasionally lift a ceremonial glass or clink the sides of glasses to toast others, but except for the best man at a wedding, that's about all that is involved.

There: Toasting is more common in other parts of the world. It is also often more elaborate, and more important. To avoid embarrassment, North Americans should first learn the local toasting customs in advance and carry along a short repertoire of clever, all-purpose toasts to draw from on a moment's notice.

13. ENTERING A CROWDED AISLE OF SEATED PEOPLE

Here: At sporting events or the theater, North Americans usually slide into a crowded aisle while facing *forward*, with their backsides to the people already seated in that aisle.

There: In the Soviet Union and a scattering of other European countries, one enters an aisle *facing* the people already seated; to do otherwise is considered quite rude. To follow the correct local practice, just watch how others are doing it.

14. "I SEE A PRETTY GIRL"

Here: North Americans signal this message by wiggling the eyebrows up and down, and perhaps whistling.

There: Italians convey this same message by screwing a stiff index finger into the cheek. Greeks stroke their chins, the French kiss their fingertips, and Brazilians form an imaginary telescope with their hands and then direct it at the object of beauty.

15. WHISTLING

Here: North Americans whistle at pretty women, but also as a form of cheering at sporting events, and while applauding an outstanding performance. In these situations, it is a signal of approval.

There: Throughout Europe, however, whistling at such public events means just the opposite: a signal of disapproval, even derision.

16. NODDING AND SHAKING THE HEAD

Here: Throughout most of the world, nodding the head up and down signifies "Yes" and shaking it back and forth means "No."

✓↑ *There:* In Bulgaria, however, the custom is just the opposite. There, to signal "No" they nod the head up and down; and to indicate "Yes" they shake the head back and forth.

17. "YOU HAVE A TELEPHONE CALL"

Here: North Americans would probably send this signal by first forming a fist, then extending the thumb and little finger widely to simulate a telephone, and finally, holding it up to the ear. But this is not a universally understood signal.

There: In Argentina, for example, the accepted hand motion is to extend the forefinger and make a circular motion near the temple or ear— probably a vestige of the old hand-cranked telephones. (But, to North Americans and to Germans, this also is the signal for saying "That's crazy!")

18. SIGNALING MEASUREMENTS

Here: Ask a North American "How long is six inches?" and he or she will probably hold out two stiff forefingers and separate them by an approximate distance of six inches.

There: In Colombia, however, using the forefingers in this manner is considered a very rude gesture. As a result, Colombians prefer a different system for gesturing both distances and heights. For distances, they will hold the hand and forearm out stiffly and take the cutting edge of the other palm to mark off the desired distance. For heights, holding the hand out with palm pointed downward is used to designate the height of *animals* only; to designate the height of a *human,* the palm is held vertically.

19. KNOCKING ON A DOOR

Here: In North American homes, bathroom doors are customarily left partially open. That way, we know it is not occupied.

There: In European homes, bathroom doors are customarily kept closed. Therefore, in European homes, always knock on the door first. One important footnote for Mexico: There you should avoid rapping on a door with the often-used "dum-de-de-dum-dum . . . dum-dum" (or rapping to the old musical phrase "Shave and a haircut, two bits.") In Mexico, this particular series of beats carries a very crude and rude message.

20. FINALLY, SLAPPING THE FIST UPWARD INTO THE OTHER PALM

Here: A North American might be seen idly swinging the arms while unconsciously slapping the fist of one hand into the palm of the other.

There: Be careful in Chile, however. This self-same gesture has only one meaning, "Up yours!"

There you have 20 tips for knowing *right* from *rude.* Carry these with you and you can alter the appellation from "Innocent Abroad" to "Savant Abroad."

6

Country-by-
Country Listing

Try this experiment: Sit in an international airport, tourist attraction, or cosmopolitan hotel and try to guess the nationalities of people passing by. Some are easy, while others are all but impossible. You may feel absolutely certain that fellow over there by the wall is Norwegian . . . but he turns out to be Greek.

The same play of clues and obstacles holds true with gestures and body language. Cataloging gestures around the world is like trying to catalog faces among the races of the world. There are the easy ones, the inconsistencies, and the surprises.

Even within a country, there may not be total agreement about the exact meaning of each gesture. For example, here is a typical comment from one cultural attaché when reviewing the listing for his country:

> There is no such thing as a universal attitude in my country on, for example, touching or not touching, and therefore (gestures) are hard to categorize. However, the common gestures you illustrate are (known and understood).

So, as you read through this country-by-country listing, or as you hop-scotch from one to another, bear in mind that these are the gestures in *general* use, but there may always be exceptions. Unfortunately, there is no definitive encyclopedia of gestures for all nationalities or countries. In fact, in my years of research, I came across only two countries (Brazil and The Netherlands) with reference books totally devoted to describing common gestures in use there.

If you are going to, say, Argentina it might be a good idea to examine not only the gestures for that country but also to skim the list of common gestures for neighboring countries. Gestures cross borders easily, and this skimming process will help you get a "feel" for prevailing customs.

In the world of gestures, the best single piece of advice is to remember the two "As"—"ask" and be "aware." If you see a motion or gesture that is new or confusing, *ask* a local person what it signifies. Then, during the rest of your visit, be *aware* of the many body signs and customs around you.

Use this topic of gestures as a gambit in conversation during your visit. When visiting another country, I frequently nudge social conversation toward the subject of gestures and body language. For example, one good conversational opener is "What is the proper way to beckon a waiter in your country?" The response may be "Oh, we gesture to a waiter this way. (Demonstrates.) But why?" Then, you venture further: "I'm interested in different gestures and body language around the world. I'm interested in knowing what unusual gestures you have here in your country." Your companion will probably counter with "Oh, we don't have any unusual gestures." But what they are really saying is that their gestures are not strange or unusual *to them.*

At this point, you can mention some of the oddities and anomalies around the world, such as the different interpretations given to the "O.K." sign, or the "V for victory" sign. They'll catch on quickly. Best of all, they'll then want to know about "strange and unusual gestures" in *your* country.

Thus, the international communications gap narrows. Above all, remember that behavior is a fickle business. There are no absolutes. There is no single, comprehensive rule book for human behavior or nonverbal communication.

In summary, use the following listings as general guidelines . . . but also be "aware" and then, when in doubt, "ask."

EUROPE

Austria

- Shaking hands is the customary greeting, and it is done when meeting and leaving. A lady will often offer her hand in greeting, and it is polite to shake hands with the lady first, before the men who are also present.

- Handshakes will be firm, with direct eye contact.

- Austrian men may kiss a woman's hand when meeting. They may also enter a restaurant ahead of a woman—the purpose being to determine if the place is proper for a lady to enter.

- Men should rise when a woman enters the room.

- Prolonged touching, closeness, or back-slapping are not common among new or casual acquaintances.

- Chewing gum in public is considered inappropriate.

- Hands in pockets when conversing should be avoided.

- Stroking an imaginary beard signifies that someone's comment is old and worn.

- Austrians keep the fork in the left hand when eating and push food on to it with the knife.

- Beckoning a waiter or some other person is done by simply raising the hand with the index finger extended.

- Keep your hands above the table when dining, with wrists or perhaps forearms resting on the table. Placing your hands in your lap during a meal is considered rude.

- Avoid cutting fish or potatoes with your knife; it suggests they are tough. A special fish knife is often provided when eating fish.

- Place your knife and fork next to your plate when you finish eating.

- To signify good luck, make two fists (thumbs tucked inside the fist) and gesture as if you are pounding lightly on a table.

- To signal "one," use the upright thumb.

- On highways, a rude German gesture may be seen in which the forefinger is twisted or screwed into the temple of the head. It means "You're a crazy driver!"

- Many of the gestures pictured in Chapter 2 are known in Austria. Examples: "O.K." sign, thumbs up, forearm jerk, "the finger," and "V" for victory.

Belgium

- Shaking hands is the common greeting, perhaps with a light pressure and briefly, not prolonged. If a woman wishes to shake hands, she will extend hers first.

- Handshakes are exchanged on both meeting and departing.

- When close friends meet, they may kiss cheeks. Remember, this is a *gesture*—not the real thing! No wet kisses. A light brushing of cheeks, a pursing of the lips—that's all. In Belgium, this is often done *three* times: (1) one cheek, (2) over to the other, and (3) back to the first.

- Pointing with the index finger is considered impolite.

- Snapping your fingers when others are present is also frowned upon.

- Standing with your hand or hands in your pockets while conversing is considered bad manners.

- Men allow women to enter rooms, board buses, and so on, in advance and also rise when women enter a room.

- Back-slapping or being noisy are considered rude actions.

- When dining, keep your wrists on the table; don't place them in your lap.

- Belgians customarily eat "Continental Style"—with the fork constantly in the left hand.

- Casualness may be regarded as rudeness. So, use good posture, never put your feet on chairs or tables, and yawning or scratching or using a toothpick in public are all considered poor manners. Same with blowing one's nose or sneezing—try to do them away from others.

- Many of the "Most Popular Gestures" described in Chapter 2 are known in Belgium.

Bulgaria

- The handshake is the customary form of greeting for both men and women.

- Bulgaria is much like the United States when it comes to touching and closeness. Physical contact is limited to such things as good male friends occasionally patting one another on the back, and good female or male-female friends greeting each other with the so-called "cheek kiss," which is actually just a brushing of the cheeks.

- As in many European countries, it is the custom when dining to rest both wrists on the table. Exceptions will be seen in

Bulgaria, depending on the individual and the setting, but a general practice is to not keep one or both hands in the lap. (One explanation for this habit is provided under the listing for Switzerland.)

- While eating, it's O.K. to sop up gravy with your bread, but use your fork rather than your fingers, of course.

- A rarity here is that nodding the head up and down means "no" instead of "yes" as in most parts of the world. Therefore, to say "yes" a Bulgarian will shake the head back and forth. Got it? (If so, shake your head back and forth—that means "yes.")

- Putting the forefinger to the temple and rotating it back and forth means someone is "crazy."

- As in most European countries, most of the gestures pictured and described in Chapter 2 will be known here, with these special notations: (1) the "forearm jerk" is a sexual insult but, in a way, it also means "You are not going to have your way as far as I'm concerned," (2) the "V for victory" can also be used to signal the number "two," (3) the vertical or "hook 'em horns" gesture is not generally known, and (4) the "fig" is less of an insult and usually connotes "You are going to get nothing; I will not let you have your way."

Czechoslovakia

- Whether in formal or informal settings, do the round of shaking hands with everyone present on both arrival and departure.

- Czechoslovakians are not considered strong "touchers," except perhaps among artistic circles when casual acquaintances might hug when greeting.

- The hitch-hiking gesture, using the upright thumb, is known but a more commonly used motion is to wave the outstretched arm up and down.

- Never applaud in a church, whether the occasion is a wedding, concert, or whatever.

- Toasting is fairly common, but wait for the host to begin.

- As in Bulgaria and certain other countries, the signal to indicate something or someone is "crazy" is to take the stiff forefinger and "screw" it into the temple of the head.

- Czechs may not put their knife and fork down while eating, except of course when using a napkin or becoming involved in a lively dinner conversation.

- To signal you've finished eating, place the knife and fork in parallel at one side of the plate. To signal you're just pausing, place them in a criss-cross position on the plate.

- Avoid putting your elbows on the dining table.

- Czechs will be acquainted with most of the popular gestures shown and described in Chapter 2, but it's always worthwhile to inquire about any special nuances in their country.

Denmark

- A firm, fairly short handshake is customary. Children will often offer their hand in greeting and are taught to make direct eye contact and even bow slightly when meeting a hostess for the first time. When meeting a couple, shake hands with the woman first. If you are seated, be certain to rise to shake hands.

- Like most North Europeans, Danes are friendly but not overly expressive physically.

- Politeness is very important. For example, going through a door is a ceremony in itself: women always go first, and men should allow their host to hold the door. Going up stairways, gentlemen always go first; down, ladies go first. At theaters, when entering the aisle always face the people who are already seated.

- Formal dinners are fairly common in Denmark, so consider bringing appropriate clothes. Also, a card will be presented to each man with the name of the female dining partner who will be seated on his right. After being introduced to that woman, you should escort her to the table at the proper time.

- When going to restaurants, the man customarily takes charge. Waiters are signaled by simply raising the hand and index finger.

- Toasting is common and popular. Wait for the host to begin. Before sipping, look around at the group or toast one person directly, then sip and once again gain eye contact.

- Don't get up from the dining table until the host or hostess does.

- When driving, a gesture of contempt is to point the index finger at the temple and rotate it back and forth.

- Danes will recognize most of the more popular gestures described in Chapter 2.

England, Scotland and Wales (The United Kingdom)

- Whereas on the European continent handshaking is done when meeting and departing, day in and day out and even with the same assortment of acquaintances, in these three countries it is done less frequently.

- Summon waiters at restaurants by raising the hand. To signal that you would like the check (called "the bill" there), make a motion with both hands as if you were signing your name on paper.

- In Scotland, unlike many European countries, eating on the street is considered acceptable.

- Loud conversations and any form of boisterousness in public places should be avoided.

- Avoid staring at someone in public. Privacy is highly valued and respected in these countries.

- The "queue" or line of people is considered almost sacred. You must never "jump the queue," meaning to butt or push your way into a line of waiting people.

- In Wales, when addressing a group, speakers should avoid rubbing their noses, standing with hands in pockets, or shuffling the feet.

- In England, holding the nose and then pulling on an imaginary chain is a signal for "It stinks," and is something of an insult.

- Plan on meeting the Queen? Better be well prepared. When meeting royalty, the custom of bowing and curtsying is optional for outsiders. However, for men a slight inclination of the head would be appropriate and appreciated, and women should curtsy by slightly bending one knee. As for handshaking with royalty, the rule is that the first move will be made by them. Never actually touch the Queen, even to gently guide her in some direction. And don't offer to shake her hand unless she extends her hand to you first.

- If you smoke, it is the custom to offer cigarettes to others in your conversational group before lighting up.

- When drinking socially in British pubs, after paying for a drink, pick up your change. To leave it there (as is often the custom in the United States) could imply that you are leaving it as a tip.

- Other common practices: when yawning, cover the mouth; use handkerchiefs discreetly; remove hats when entering a building; men should cross their legs at the knees rather than placing one ankle across the other knee; women usually cross them at the ankles—in fact, watch for news photos of the Queen or other prominent women there and you'll note that when seated, they usually use the prim, Victorian manner of crossing them at the ankles.

- Most of the gestures in Chapter 2 will be known, but pay special attention to the "V" for victory gesture. In these countries, it is done with the *palm facing outward;* to reverse the hand, with the palm facing yourself, signals "Up Yours!" and is obviously rude and offensive.

- To repeat, politeness and good manners are expected and appreciated.

Finland

- The custom here is that both men and women will shake hands when introduced, or when meeting. Even children will often shake hands upon meeting guests.

- When greeting someone at a distance, a raised hand or tip of the hat is common. Also, men remove their hats when meeting or conversing, or when entering a home, church, or elevator.

- Bear hugs and cheek-kissing, so well-known just across the border in the Soviet Union, are neither common nor popular in Finland. Emotions are not expressed publicly, only among relatives and very good friends.

- It is inappropriate to eat food while walking on the street. The only exception might be ice cream.

- The European style of eating—fork remaining in the left hand—prevails in Finland. Avoid eating anything with your fingers, including fruit.

- Refrain from eating before your host begins, and take small portions because it is the custom to eat everything on one's plate.

- When conversing, direct eye contact is important.

- Crossing the legs at the knees is preferred over crossing them ankle-at-the-knee.

- At a dinner party, it is customary to refrain from drinking until the host offers a toast.

- When passing the salt during dinner, it is bad luck to deliver it hand-to-hand. Instead, put the salt shaker down on the table and let the next person pick it up.

- Standing with arms folded is sometimes viewed as a sign of arrogance.

- Always cover the mouth when yawning.

- Many of the gestures explained in Chapter 2 will be known in Finland, although not necessarily practiced.

France

- The mode of handshaking is usually as follows: a light, quick, single handshake, which is done with great frequency (arrivals, departures, each and every day). A strong, pumping handshake is considered uncultured. Also, when entering a room, greet each person in the room. A French woman offers her hand first.

- Close friends and young people often kiss on either cheek (but it is really *touching* cheeks and "kissing the air").

- Be certain to carry a good supply of business cards, since they are exchanged often.

- Some common actions and gestures to be avoided:

  —Resting the feet on tables or chairs

  —Using toothpicks, nail clippers or combs in public

  —Conversing with hands in pockets

  —Chewing gum in public

  —Yawning or scratching in public

  —Loud conversations in public

  —Snapping the fingers of both hands, or slapping an open palm over the closed fist—both have vulgar meanings.

- Since it's not particularly polite in France to point with the hand and fingers, when you want to beckon a waiter it's best to tip the head back slightly and just say *garçon* ("waiter").

- To call a taxi, many Parisians will simply snap their fingers.

- When seated, the French customarily cross the legs at the knees. Good posture and decorum are virtues in France.

- Some unique gestures in France:

  —Forming a circle with your thumb and forefinger and placing it over your nose, and then twisting; this signals that "someone is drunk."

  —The "O.K." sign (thumb and forefinger forming a circle) in some parts of France signifies "zero" or "worthless."

  —Here the "V" for victory signal is done with palm *either* forward or backward; both mean "peace" or "victory." (In England, the "V" is *only* done with the palm outward; if the palm faces inward it is an obscene gesture.)

  —Playing an imaginary flute is a way of signaling that someone is talking on and on and becoming tiresome.

  —On French highways, if another driver raises his hand in the air, fingers up, and rotates it back and forth, it means he is not happy with your driving.

- Always use a tissue or handkerchief when sneezing, and be as discreet as possible when blowing your nose.

- When dining, the French use the "continental" style, with fork constantly in the left hand. Also, rest your wrists lightly on the table, and do not put your hands in your lap. Other dining practices:

  —Bread or rolls are broken and eaten with the fingers and placed next to your dinner plate, usually directly on the table-cloth.

  —Fruit is peeled with a knife and eaten with a fork.

  —Lettuce and other leaf vegetables are not cut with a knife but, instead, folded into small pieces and eaten with a fork.

  —Never use bread to wipe up sauces except, perhaps, at family dinners.

  —The French find it strange to pick up sandwiches and other such foods with the fingers. It is more common to cut them with a knife and fork.

  —When you have finished eating, place the knife and fork side-by-side across your plate with the fork tines up.

- When approaching the dining table, allow your host to indicate where you should sit.

- When using the hands to count, start with a fist, palm facing you, and then lift the thumb to signify "one," then add the index finger to signal "two," and so on.

- Author and Harvard professor Laurence Wylie also offers these important and singularly Gallic gestures:

  —Pointing to the eye means "You can't fool me."

  —To say "How dull," flick the fingers across the cheek.

  —Using the index and middle fingers to push the nose upward signals "It's so easy I could do it with my fingers up my nose."

  —And when the French issue their famous shrug with the shoulders, palms extended, it means "It doesn't worry me." But if the palms are raised chest high, it becomes "What do you expect me to do about it?"

- With the few variations noted above, the French will probably be acquainted with all the other popular gestures shown in Chapter 2.

As a final word on actions and physical behavior in France, just remember that the word "etiquette" is derived from French.

Germany

- A fairly firm handshake is the custom among men, often with just one or two "pumps." Children and women will often offer their hand in greeting, too. Cheek-kissing is rare.

- Business cards are exchanged frequently.

- Shaking hands with the other hand in a pocket is considered impolite. For this reason, small children are chastised for putting their hands in their pockets because it is considered disrespectful.

- When arriving to meet a group of people, shake hands with each and every person.

- Men rise when a woman enters the room, or when conversing with a woman. On the other hand, women may remain seated.

- Never open a closed door without knocking first.

- When acknowledging or signaling "thanks" to a crowd of people, Germans will often clasp their hands together and raise them high over their heads.

- During operas or concerts, it is important to remain quiet and still. Coughing or restlessness is considered rude.

- Men enter a restaurant *before* women, unless they are elderly or of higher status. One reason is, according to the custom, the man is inspecting the restaurant to see if it is proper for a woman to enter.

- When dining in some restaurants, if there are empty seats at your table and no other free tables, the maitre d'hotel may seat others with you. This is quite common in Germany—in fact, you can do the same if you arrive and there are no single free tables. There should be no obligation to carry on a conversation with others at the table unless both parties seem so inclined.

- Never place your foot or feet on furniture.

- At dinner parties, don't drink until your host begins. When toasting, clink glasses only for special occasions, like a birthday. Men toast women, never vice versa.

- When eating: the fork is held in the left hand; don't cut potatoes, pancakes, or dumplings with a knife because that suggests they are tough; rarely, if ever, eat with your fingers—that includes fruit and even sandwiches; hard rolls are often served at breakfast, and even these should be cut with a knife, not the fingers; smoke between courses only if you see others doing so.

- A good general rule when eating is to watch and follow the actions of your German host.

- Chewing gum while conversing with another person is considered extremely impolite. As one German remarked, "To Germans it looks like a cow chewing on a cud."

- A man walks on the left side of a woman (Germans contend this is a romantic symbol because the heart is located on the left side), but on busy streets he will walk on the side where traffic is passing.

- To beckon a waiter, raise the hand with index finger extended.

- When waving goodbye, extend the hand upward, palm out, and wave the fingers up and down. Don't waggle the hand back and forth, like a semaphore because that means "no."

- To signal for quiet, place the index finger over the lips, with fingernail facing outward.

- Four special gestures in Germany:

—To signal "one," hold the thumb upright.

—On Germany's famous autobahns (highways), if one driver is unhappy with the driving of another, he may point the index finger to the temple and make a twisting or screwing motion. This is considered *very* rude, and means, in effect, "You are crazy!"

—To signal "good luck," Germans make two fists with thumbs tucked inside the other fingers and then make a motion like they are pounding lightly on a surface.

—In some parts of Germany, when people arrive at a large dinner table and it is awkward to reach across and shake hands, they will simply rap their knuckles slightly on the table as a form of greeting to the others. The same gesture

139

may apply when leaving the table ahead of the other guests. It is also used in university classrooms for students greeting professors.

- If you are driving or parking a car and you accidentally dent or scratch another car, *no matter how minor,* it is important that you contact the owner or even check with local authorities for proper procedures. Germans take great pride in their automobiles.

- Germans will probably recognize the common gestures described in Chapter 2, but make a special effort not to use the "O.K." gesture since it is considered rude in Germany.

Greece

- The Greeks are warm and friendly, and handshaking will be the same with firm grasps and good eye contact the first and every time thereafter. You may even be embraced, with a kiss on each cheek, although men do this only after long absences. Good friends may also gently slap a hand on the other's shoulder.

- A slight upward nod of the head means "no." Another version is to lift the eyebrows upward. To indicate "yes" or "of course," the Greeks may tilt the head to either side.

- Greeks not only smile when they are happy but also sometimes when they are angry or upset.

- When you compliment a Greek, he or she may issue a puff of air through pursed lips which is an old action symbolizing the warding off of the "evil eye."

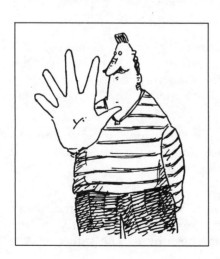

- Waving your hand palm outward and fingers spread, is not a form of greeting. In fact, in Greece it can be confused with the Greek gesture *moutza*, where the hand is extended outward, away from the body, in something of a pushing motion. This is actually an ancient rude gesture still used today in Greece.

- Like many people in the Middle East and Mediterranean areas, Greeks may casually finger "worry beads." On first sight, these appear similar to rosary beads. But they have no special religious significance and are used more as an outlet for nervous energy or as a calming influence.

- When it comes to lines, or queues, in public places the Greeks are the opposite of the British. Don't expect orderly lines.

- The "O.K." sign (index finger and thumb forming a circle) may be construed as a symbol for a body orifice, so use it with caution. It is *not* used to signify "O.K." Similarly, the "fig" gesture may be viewed as a phallic symbol, therefore obscene.

- To signal "everything is O.K.," use the "thumb's up" gesture. However, the "thumb's *down*" gesture is quite rude, the type of derisive signal you might see one bus driver flash to another when some rule of the road is broken.

- In Greece the "middle finger up" is not generally known or used. However, as in Egypt and a few other Mediterranean countries, if you hold the hand out, palm down, and extend just the middle finger downward, *that* is an obscene gesture signaling "Up yours!"

- To express the sighting of a pretty woman, a Greek will use his hand and fingers to stroke his chin. A more forward, even crude gesture is to hiss, wink, and make a kissing motion with the lips.

- To beckon someone, extend the arm, palm down, and make a scratching motion with the fingers.

- When dining, it is quite acceptable to use your fingers for the appetizers that are served before lunch or dinner. Also, Greeks may smoke cigarettes often during a meal.

- Male guests of honor usually sit to the right of the hostess, with female guests seated at the right of the host whereas, say, in the Netherlands and Sweden the male sits to the left of the hostess and the female sits to the left of the host.

- At the dining table, the spoon placed above your place is for the dessert.

- Keep your wrists on the table while dining, not in your lap. As for which foods may be taken with the fingers, just watch your host and imitate him or her.

- To signal you have finished eating, cross your utensils in an "X" shape, knife under the fork. Another signal is to put your napkin next to your plate.

- Any visitor who participates in the Greek folk dancing is offering a gesture of appreciation and friendliness.

- Many of the gestures shown in Chapter 2 will be known to the Greeks but not necessarily used. For example, the "V for victory" is known and used (and also means "We are *first,*") but the "hook 'em horns," "thumb's up," and "middle finger" signals are not generally used. The "forearm jerk" is also known, but only because the Greeks see Europeans using it.

Hungary

- When initially meeting, departing, and upon meeting thereafter, the handshake is the customary gesture. A man usually waits for a woman to offer her hand.

- Hungarians are not considered a touching society. Two people usually stand about an arm's length apart.

- Embraces as greetings are uncommon and usually done only by good friends, maybe after long absences. They are accompanied by cheek-to-cheek contact.

- At formal parties, wait to be introduced. At informal parties, introduce yourself.

- Men customarily walk to the left of women, or of any honored guest.

- Hungarians use their eating utensils in the Continental style: fork remaining in the left hand at all times.

- Keep both hands above the table, with neither one or both in your lap.

- Many of the popular gestures shown in Chapter 2 will be known in Hungary, but it is best to check specific meanings with a local friend before using them freely. For example, the "V for victory" is not common and the "fig" gesture signifies "You won't get (something)."

Ireland

- A relatively firm and straightforward handshake is the custom in both Northern Ireland and the Republic of Ireland.

- Business cards are not exchanged as formally as in other European countries.

- Physical contact is not common among those in Northern Ireland, except between very good friends.

- Also in the North, women are seated first. The more formal Irish will not cross their legs with one ankle over the knee, but prefer instead to cross them at the ankles or one knee over the other knee.

- It's difficult to offend anyone in Ireland by innocently using the wrong fork or forgetting to shake hands at the right moment, so don't worry too much about it.

- One travel writer advises that the most offensive gesture in Ireland is failing to buy a round of drinks when it is your turn. Similarly, refusing a drink (except for health reasons) may be considered rude.

- Queues (lines of people) are common and respected, so don't barge into the middle of a line of waiting people.

- Generally, while the Irish have a worldwide reputation as being friendly, hearty people, they are not especially demonstrative with gestures or other body language.

- Most of the popular gestures shown in Chapter 2 will be known in Ireland, and especially the offensive "reverse V for victory" gesture.

Italy

- Shake hands when meeting and departing, no matter how brief or often the encounter.

- Italians are known for more physical contact than other Europeans: cheek kissing among good acquaintances, embraces between men who are good friends, lingering handshakes with the other hand over your hand or at the elbow, and so on. You might also observe two Italian men walking along arm-in-arm.

- Women should cover their heads when visiting churches. Also shorts should not be worn, nor should sleeveless or skimpy tops or blouses.

- In crowded public places, it is not considered rude to push or shove slightly. Don't be offended by this custom.

- At the dining table, the host and hostess will usually sit at opposite ends of the table with the male guest of honor seated at the left of the hostess and the female guest at the left of the host.

- Your host should pour the wine, and Italians consider it unfeminine for a woman to pour wine.

- One travel counselor advises that in Italy wine is viewed as almost a food, therefore it is rude to over-imbibe.

- Refrain from eating until your hostess begins.

- A knife and fork placed above your plate are used for dessert.

- Italians are known for being among the most demonstrative of all nationalities. One acquaintance of mine, when talking on the telephone, actually placed the phone on the table so that he could gesture more freely.

- It is best to cover the mouth when yawning.

- Shrugging the shoulders signals "I don't know" or "I don't care."

- Some specific hand gestures in Italy are these (full explanations are provided in Chapter 3):

—The chin flick

—The "hook 'em horns," or *cornuto* signifies that your mate has been unfaithful.

—The "cheek screw," to denote seeing a pretty woman

—The "hand purse"

—The "eyelid pull"

—The "forearm jerk"

—The "finger"

—The "flat hand flick" means "I don't want it, get lost."

—The "nose tap"

—To wave goodbye, palm up, fingers wagging up and down

—Tapping the hand to the forehead, like a salute, means "you're crazy."

—"Throwing the saliva," or pulling imaginary saliva from the mouth and throwing it, is a strong insult.

- Be certain to also study all the popular gestures shown

in Chapter 2, since most of these will apply—or be known—in Italy.

Netherlands

- Shaking hands always accompanies meetings and departures, for both men and woman. Children will shake hands, too. Embracing is done only among very close friends and relatives.

- Some unique gestures you may encounter in Holland:

    —Sucking the thumb signals that someone is lying, or making up a story.

    —Bending the arm at the elbow, then tapping the underside of the elbow with your other hand signifies that another person is "unreliable."

    —Patting the back of one hand with the fingers of the other hand signifies "he (or she) is gay."

    —Rubbing the nose with the forefinger from the bridge downward indicates someone is stingy or cheap.

    —Grabbing at an imaginary fly in front of your face indicates that someone else is crazy.

    —If someone places a hand under their chin and draws it downward as if shaping a long beard, it is a way of saying "That story is very old."

    —To signal across a room that someone else has a telephone call, make a circular motion around your ear with your index finger. (In many other countries that signals the person "is crazy.")

    —The Dutch signal for "that person is crazy" is to tap the center of the forehead.

    —If a person taps the thumbnails together (as if applauding), it is a signal that that person does not appreciate what has just transpired, such as a joke, song or comment.

- Be certain to wipe your feet before entering a home.

- Good, direct eye contact is important.

- Touching and other casual contact is not common, unless the parties are very close friends, and then there might be a slight embrace and even light kissing motions to each cheek.

- Like several other European countries, it is considered impolite to chew gum in front of others, or to stand with your hands in your pockets.

- When a man accompanies a woman walking along the street, it is the custom for men to walk on the side closest to the street.

- When a woman enters a room, the men usually rise.

- When dining, the hostess may serve herself first, a custom handed down from the days when the hostess tested the food to prove it was edible. Don't eat before the hostess.

- Take small portions of food, try to taste every item, and try to eat everything on your plate—not doing so may be considered impolite.

- The Dutch eat continental style, fork in the left hand, and will eat even sandwiches and fruit with a knife and fork.

- Keep both wrists above or on the table, not in your lap.

- Getting up during a meal—even to go to the bathroom—is considered rude.

- Many of the Dutch will recognize the popular gestures shown in Chapter 2, so review these signals as well.

Norway

- Handshakes are fairly brief but firm, and little other personal touching is done here, except among relatives and very close friends. Avoid putting your arm around another person, or slapping them on the back.

- If you are seated, always rise to be introduced to another person.

- Avoid speaking in a loud voice.

- A Norwegian superstition holds that, if you want to wish a fisherman good luck, you spit after him. Also, having thirteen people at a table is considered bad luck, which, like the general Western fear of the number thirteen, can probably be traced back to the Last Supper.

- When dining, the host and hostess will sit at opposite ends of the table, with the female guest at the left of the host and the male guest at the left of the hostess. Don't start eating until your host or hostess does. Norwegians eat continental style, with the fork always in the left hand, and also use a knife and fork to eat the famous Scandinavian open-faced sandwiches. It is impolite to leave immediately after dining.

- Toasting is common: make eye contact, raise the glass upward to eye level, say "*Skoal*," drink, make eye contact again, and then place the glass down.

- To beckon a waiter, raise the hand with the index finger upward. Some young people may snap the fingers, but this is considered impolite.

- Most of the popular gestures shown in Chapter 2 will be generally known in Norway, but not necessarily practiced.

Poland

- Shake hands when you are introduced, when you meet someone for the first time that day, and upon departing. Men should wait for women to extend their hand first.

- An older Pole may very well lean down to kiss the hand of a woman, especially a married woman. Visitors are not expected to emulate them. Women greet close female friends with a brief embrace and slight kisses, one on each cheek.

- Poles are not considered "touchers," so hugs and embracing are not common, people usually stand about an arm's length from each other when conversing, and there is usually no other casual body contact (e.g., touching when talking) except by very close friends.

- Poles tend to speak rather softly. Avoid chewing gum while conversing with another person.

- When dining, depending on the number of guests, the guest of honor is often seated at the head of the table. As in many European countries, when dining the hands should be kept visible and above the table, never in the lap. Refrain from eating until all others have been served. Empty your glass only if you wish a refill.

- Toasting before and during the meal is very common. The host usually begins, and you can reciprocate later.

- When a Pole flicks his finger against his neck, he is inviting you to join him in a drink (usually vodka). This is a very common gesture, but used only among very close friends, otherwise it may be considered rude.

- Most of the gestures discussed in Chapter 2 will at least be recognized in Poland, but be aware which are used and what they mean. For example, the "V for victory" signal is often seen in connection with the Solidarity labor movement. Also, whereas the "fig" gesture is considered obscene in places like Greece and elsewhere, in Poland it says, in effect "In the end you will get nothing." Finally, the "hook 'em horns" or vertical horns gesture is generally neither used nor known in Poland.

Portugal

- As in many Latin countries, a warm and firm handshake is the rule here. When meeting close friends, shaking hands is not necessary; instead, men may pat or slap each other on the back, and women may embrace and kiss cheeks.

- The Portuguese are not overly demonstrative with hand gestures or body language.

- To wave or get someone's attention, the Portuguese will extend the arm upward, palm out, and wag the fingers up and down, as if patting someone on the head.

- To signal that everything is going well, the Portuguese use the "thumbs up" gesture, sometimes using both hands (and thumbs).

- An unusual gesture in Portugal tells your hostess that you really enjoyed dinner. To do this, at the end of a meal kiss the side of your index finger and then pinch your earlobe between the kissed index finger and the thumb.

- The "chin flick" has a different meaning than in Italy, where it shows impatience, even disgust. In Portugal, brushing your fingers (palm inward) off the bottom of your chin and away from your face signals "I don't know the answer." The same motion using the thumb means that something no longer exists, or something died.

- Portuguese eat by holding the fork in the left hand at all times. To signal they have finished eating, they will place the knife and fork vertically on the plate. They rarely eat with their hands— even fruit is eaten with a knife and fork.

- Don't use bread or parts of a dinner roll to sop up gravy or juices. Before leaving the table, fold your napkin and place it beside your plate.

- As in other European countries, many of the more popular gestures explained and illustrated in Chapter 2 will be recognized in Portugal, although not all of them will be put to daily use.

Romania

- A traditional, firm handshake is the custom here but done frequently—on meeting, on departing, and even when meeting the same person several times in a short period of time.

- Men rise when meeting a woman, but the woman need not rise to be introduced.

- A Romanian man may lightly kiss the hand of a woman he is meeting, but outsiders should not feel obliged to adopt that custom. Very good friends and relatives will embrace and kiss cheeks.

- Business cards are freely exchanged.

- Women visiting a Greek Orthodox Church should dress conservatively, with bare arms covered and skirts rather than slacks. They need not cover their heads, however.

- When dining, several toasts will be exchanged. Romanians eat with the fork in the left hand, keep hands above the table, and keep the napkin alongside the plate rather than in the lap.

- Most of the popular gestures from Chapter 2 will be known, with two important notes: the "fig" gesture is a sexual insult and the "vertical horns" gesture signifies being cuckolded.

Spain

- Handshakes are warm and friendly in Spain, often accompanied by a light pat on the back. As in many Latin countries, the *abrazo* (embrace) is common among male friends. Women do the same: a slight embrace, and the motion of kissing each cheek. Men and women always shake hands when meeting.

- Men usually wait for all women in a room to be seated before they sit down.

- The "O.K." sign, with thumb and forefinger in a circle and the other fingers splayed outward, is an obscene gesture in Spain.

- The "thumb's up" gesture has taken on political implications in Spain. It can mean support for the Basque separatist movement; therefore, it is popular in the North of Spain where the Basques reside, but in other parts it might be regarded as provocative.

- Local residents sometimes push and shove when in line for taxis, phones, hotel registrations, and other such public situations, but tourists are often respected.

- When seated before an audience, no matter how small, yawning or stretching is considered inappropriate.

- When seated, Spanish men usually cross their legs at the knees; it is considered "unladylike" for women to cross their legs.

- Eye contact is important. But women should be wary of eye contact with strangers or new acquaintances since it signals interest. A Spaniard with "snapping eyes" is exhibiting either anger or impatience.

- The Spanish use many arm and head gestures. Hands should not be placed in the pockets when conversing, and gum chewing in public is considered rude.

- To beckon someone, stretch out the arm and hand, palm downward, and make a scratching motion toward your body with the fingers. Another way to call a waiter is to say "psssst," which locals may do but is considered somewhat rude if done by tourists.

- When dining, many special continental customs apply: Guests of honor are seated at the host's right; eating is done with the fork constantly in the left hand; never use your fingers to push food on to your utensils; keep your wrists on the table and avoid putting your hands in your lap; and to indicate you've finished eating, place the knife and fork in parallel across the plate—placing them on opposite sides of the plate can be interpreted as saying "I would like some more."

- Review Chapter 2, "The Most Popular Gestures," because many of these will be known and used in Spain.

Sweden

- As in other Nordic countries, handshaking is the common greeting, done with a firm grip and one or two pumps. No other touching is done, however, such as the bearhugs of Russia, or elbow touching associated with Latin countries. Swedes usually shake hands on arriving and departing and with every member of a group or family.

- When outdoors, Swedish men will often tip their hats when greeting a woman and remove the hat when standing to converse with a woman.

- Good eye contact when conversing is important.

- Queues are respected, so avoid barging into the middle of a line of waiting people.

- Swedes are not physically demonstrative, and excessive gesturing is not common. Don't put your hands in your pockets when conversing with people.

- When dining, the male guest of honor is seated to the left of the hostess, and the female guest of honor to the right of the host.

- Toasting is done frequently in Sweden. The procedure is to lift your glass, make eye contact all around or with one particular person, say *"Skoal,"* drink, make eye contact again, and bring the glass back to the table. The host makes the first toast. The older and more traditional way of toasting was "To lift the glass from the seventh button down on the waistcoat up to the eyes . . ." and then follow the procedure just described.

- When leaving someone's home, wait until you get to the doorway or step outside before putting on your coat. To do so earlier suggests you are anxious to leave.

- Swedes eat with the fork in the left hand, pushing morsels of food on to the back of the tines with the knife.

- Most of the popular gestures shown in Chapter 2 will be known in Sweden, but not all of them will be used.

151

Switzerland

- Since Switzerland is an amalgam of French, Italian, and German nationalities, customs from all three of those countries will be seen. For example, the German-type greeting tends to be shorter, firmer, and with no other body touching. The Italian and French influence will be seen when good friends add an embrace and even cheek-kissing. In all cases, though, shake hands with everyone present on arriving or departing and even with children.

  ^ part ? [handwritten annotation — "a part?" with caret inserted before "touching"]

- Presenting and exchanging business cards is an important custom, so carry a good supply.

- Good posture is considered an attribute in Switzerland. Crossing the legs is common, but not stretching them out; nor is slouching in your chair. However, when standing or waiting in line, be prepared for some amount of pushing and shoving.

- Be cautious about any form of littering. The Swiss take pride in tidiness and cleanliness, so any acts of littering are severely frowned upon.

- The Swiss are especially considerate about helping elderly people—alighting from buses, getting up to give them a seat, or helping them with luggage or other parcels.

- When dining, guests of honor are usually seated at the middle point of the table. Also when dining, keep your hands above the table, perhaps resting the wrists there. (A Swiss diplomat once told me this custom dates back to the sixteenth century when it was customary for hosts to provide female companions for guests and therefore keeping the hands under the table indicated that you were, let us say, enjoying her company. It evolved that when a person kept his hands beneath the table it was an indication of sexual hanky-panky.)

- Don't smoke at the dinner table.

- A popular Swiss dish is *fondue,* where a chafing dish is placed in the center of the table containing melted cheese or hot gravy and meat. Those around the table use long forks to dip pieces of bread into the cheese or gravy. One tradition is that if you drop your bread into the communal dish you must buy the wine; another version is that you must kiss all the members of the opposite sex at the table.

- As in Germany, when dining in a restaurant, don't be surprised if strangers approach and seat themselves at unused seats at your table. It is not necessary to strike up a conversation, incidentally.

- Most of the popular gestures described in Chapter 2 will be known—although not all of them necessarily practiced.

Turkey

- The standard handshake applies here, but old friends may also clasp both hands over yours or even embrace while kissing both cheeks. On arriving at an office or other gathering, shake hands with each and every person.

- Showing the sole of your shoe, or inadvertently pointing it toward someone is an insult. That is because the shoe sole is the lowest part of the body and something usually soiled and dirty.

- Ask permission before smoking, but it is considered impolite to smoke or eat while on public streets.

- Show respect to elders. Speaking in a loud voice is considered ill-mannered.

- The "fig" gesture with hand clenched in a fist and the thumb protruding between the first two fingers, is a rude gesture in Turkey.

- A gesture unique to Turkey is a way of signaling that "something is good," done by holding the hand up, palm outward, and slowly bringing the fingers into the thumb, in a grasping motion.

- Men in Turkey will be seen holding and fingering loops of beads. These are called "worry beads," used for relieving tension and have no special religious significance.

- Raising the head slightly, tipping it backward, and closing the eyes usually means "no" in Turkey.

- It is considered rude to cross your arms over your chest while conversing with someone. The same is true of putting your hands in your pockets.

- Remove your shoes when entering a Turkish mosque, and many Turkish homes.

- Signs of affection—hugging, holding hands, kissing—are usually not done in public. It is common, however, especially in rural areas, for women who are casual acquaintances to kiss one another when meeting and parting.

- Turkish women will usually not converse with a man until they have been formally introduced.

- Female visitors to Turkey should avoid traveling about unaccompanied.

- Before taking photographs, ask permission—especially in mosques or of individuals.

- When dining, Turks keep the fork in the left hand and push food on to it with the knife. Avoid eating with the fingers. If you are offered a toothpick after dining, it is O.K. to use it, but be certain to cover your mouth with the other hand.

- Among the popular gestures described in Chapter 2, here are the pertinent interpretations in Turkey: the "forearm jerk" (page 36) implies "strength" rather than being a sexual insult; the "V" signal tends to mean "two" rather than "victory"; the "O.K." circle made with thumb and forefinger signifies "homosexuality"; the "thumbs up" gesture means "O.K."; and the vertical "hook 'em horns" (page 53) gesture is not generally known or used.

Yugoslavia

- A firm handshake is the custom for both sexes, although a man should wait for the woman to extend her hand first. Close friends and relatives will greet each other with slight embraces and kisses on the cheeks. Even when staying in a private home, you may find that people will shake your hand each morning and evening.

- A greeting among homosexuals is to shake hands while pressing the middle finger into the palm.

- It is best to dress conservatively, especially women.

- The "O.K." sign means something is "perfect" or "exact" or "it's super."

- The "fig" gesture is *not* considered especially rude, as in some other Mediterranean countries. Here it symbolizes "zero" or "nothing" as when a parent might signal to a child "No, you may not have any ice cream."

- The "thumb's up" gesture means "O.K." and is also commonly used for hitch-hiking.

- Forming a fist and holding it head-high can have two meanings. If the fingers are shown outward (as in the "black power" gesture, it means "Victory!" However, if the knuckles on the back of the hand point outward, it is a gesture showing strong anger and signals "Up yours!"

- Two common gestures described and pictured in this book should be avoided in Yugoslavia because they could be interpreted as rude, even obscene. The "hook 'em horns" gesture means "Up yours," especially when the fingers point toward the person in question. The second one involves slapping the palm of one hand downward on top of the fist of the other hand.

- Another obscene gesture found in some Mediterranean countries is known and used in Yugoslavia. It is when a person holds his hand out, palm down, and extends the middle finger downward.

- The "forearm jerk," as in many countries, means "Up yours!" but for added emphasis a person in Yugoslavia may not only hit the crook of his bent elbow but the shoulder as well.

- The "eyelid pull" means "nothing," as when one tour guide might signal to another "I received no tip."

- The "hand purse," so common in Italy, is known in Yugoslavia to mean "It's good" as when conveying "This food is so good."

- To beckon a waiter, merely raise your hand. But never beckon a person by using the index finger in a curling motion. That is used only to beckon animals.

- The middle finger extended is not generally used nor known in Yugoslavia.

- When dining, it is the custom here to keep the fork in the left hand at all times, pushing the food on to it using the knife.

- To indicate you have finished eating, place the knife and fork across the center of the plate.

- Keep both wrists on or above the table while eating; it is not considered polite to place one or both hands in the lap, as is the custom in the United States and certain other countries.

- Women visitors should avoid making eye contact with or smiling at strange men while walking in public.

- Many of the gestures shown in Chapter 2 will be known and recognized, but with the exceptions and variations in meaning explained above.

U.S.S.R. (Soviet Union)

- A good, firm handshake along with direct eye contact is the customary greeting. In many parts of the Soviet Union, among close friends the "Russian bearhug" is common and is often accompanied by two or three quick kisses to alternate cheeks— even among men—and sometimes with one kiss directly on the lips. There are exceptions to this practice, however. For example, in our survey of the Uzbekistan Republic, the reply was as brief as it was clear: "No kisses."

- Bear in mind that the U.S.S.R. is composed of 15 very diverse republics with strong cultural differences. As a result, certain gestures and body language may have local flavors and meanings.

- At public gatherings, when people whistle it is a signal of disagreement and disapproval. (Again, my respondent in Uzbekistan provided a cryptic footnote here which said: "Not now.")

- Another important taboo in public gatherings might occur in a theater. As you enter the aisle to occupy your seat, if you must pass in front of others, *always* turn and face them. Never pass in front of seated people in a theater with your back to them.

- The "O.K. sign" is an ambiguous gesture, here. While as an import from the West it is known to mean "O.K.," in some parts of the Soviet Union it may be interpreted as a vulgar gesture.

- Shaking the raised fist shows disagreement and anger. The "thumbs up" sign signifies approval.

- When dining, the Russians keep the fork in the left hand and the knife in the right. Also, keep your hands out of the lap while eating; instead, rest the wrists lightly on the table. However, research indicates this might be considered an "old-fashioned" practice in some parts.

- To beckon a waiter in a restaurant, a slight nod of the head should do the job; if not just raise the hand and finger.

- Long, orderly lines of people are a common occurrence in daily lives, so be polite and respectful when joining one. Never butt into a line.

- Visitors claim that the Russian people, especially in Moscow, do not seem to smile much in public gatherings or while walking along the street. On the other hand, in smaller private gatherings, the Russian people may be more open, more friendly and may smile more often. Also, some Russians are not afraid to show emotions when in private situations. People of the same sex may be seen embracing, weeping and kissing in these situations.

- Review the list of "most popular gestures" in Chapter 2. Most of these will be known, but not necessarily used daily, in the U.S.S.R. For example, the "V for victory" may be recognized as a Western gesture, but not used in the U.S.S.R. The vertical horns (see page 53) may signify a curse, and the "fig" (see page 87) usually means "nothing" as in "You will get nothing" rather than the vulgar interpretation in Greece and other places.

MID-EAST AND AFRICA

Gestures throughout the vast African continent and the culturally complex Middle East vary because of the huge distances and many different nationalities residing there. Nonetheless, here are some general guidelines for the most heavily visited countries. This listing provides key gestures and body language as a foundation to learning more as you visit these countries.

The Arab World

The so-called Arab World consists of about 20 countries stretching from Mauritania in the West to Oman in the East. Within that area is a diverse group of people bound together primarily by language and religion—and, some would add, by oil. While religion is a strong common denominator, adherence ranges from very strict and fundamentalist to very loose and liberal. The same spectrum applies to gestures and body language: some rules and actions are adhered to strictly, others less so.

Some general customs one might observe when visiting this region include:

- Sit properly, without slouching or putting feet up on a table or other furniture. When standing and conversing, avoid leaning against a wall or standing with your hands in your pockets; both are considered disrespectful.

- Avoid showing the sole of the shoe, or inadvertently pointing it at someone. The shoe soles are the lowest and dirtiest part of the body, and therefore it is rude to point them at someone.

- Arab men will be seen fingering loops of beads that resemble a Catholic rosary. But for Arabs, many of whom are Muslim, these are tension relievers called "worry beads" and have little or no religious significance.

- The right hand prevails: eat with it, present gifts with it, touch with it. The left hand is generally regarded as the "unclean" hand and is used primarily for bodily hygiene.

- Shaking hands is important, although the grip may be less firm than Europeans and Americans use.

- Arab males are considered a "touching society." Handshakes may be prolonged, elbows may be grasped, and two men may even hold hands while walking on the street.

- When two men converse, they will probably stand much closer than Westerners. On the other hand, men should not touch an Arabic woman unless she extends her hand first.

- Long, direct eye contact among men is important. In fact, staring is not necessarily considered rude or impolite.

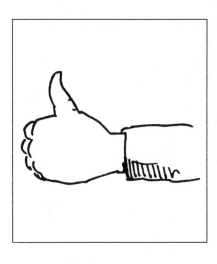

- People should not be photographed without their permission.

- Public displays of affection are frowned upon.

- Gesturing "No" is often done by tilting the head backward and either raising the eyebrows, jutting out the chin, or making a clicking sound with the tongue.

- The "thumbs up" gesture usually means "Very good. I am winning."

- Keep household pets away from visiting Arabs. Most Arabs do not like to be touched by or in the presence of such pets, especially dogs.

Some specific comments for specific Middle Eastern and African nations follow.

Egypt

- Handshakes are customary, but perhaps not with as firm a grip as Americans and Europeans use. Greetings will be warm and expressive because Egyptians believe personal relationships are important.

- Space relationships among males will be closer than Americans and Europeans are accustomed to. They will tend to stand close, and moving away may be misinterpreted as aloofness. In contrast, people of the opposite sex stand farther apart than in the United States or Europe.

- Men tend to be more touch oriented as well, and therefore a handshake may be accompanied by a gentle touching of your elbow with the other hand.

- The right hand only should be used for eating. Throughout most of the Middle East, it is the custom to reserve the left hand for bodily hygiene.

- Many Middle Easterners have what Americans and Europeans consider as "languid eyes." It appears to many outsiders that the eyelids are half closed, but this does *not* necessarily signal disinterest or disrespect.

- It is best not to sit cross-legged, because showing the sole of your shoe to another person is considered an insult.

- Many Egyptian women observe the tradition of having their husbands walk slightly ahead of them.

- Tapping the two index fingers together (side-by-side) can be considered as a crude signal that says "Would you like to sleep with me?"

- Smoking in public places is very common, and it is polite to offer your cigarettes to others present.

- When dining, it is considered impolite to eat everything on your plate. Leaving food on the plate is a symbol of abundance and a compliment to your host.

- Western eating habits prevail here, but tradition recommends that finger food be eaten only with the right hand.

Ghana

- Western-style greetings are known and used here, but this country is composed of many different ethnic groups, each with its own distinct language, customs, and culture.

- Children are trained not to look adults in the eye since this is considered an act of defiance.

- When eating, Western etiquette is practiced in Ghana.

Iran

- Handshaking is the customary form of greeting. Like most of the Arab nations, however, it may be done with a lighter grip. Good friends may greet each other with a slight embrace and a gesture of cheek kissing.

- People of the same sex will tend to stand close together when meeting and conversing.

- Shaking hands with a child shows respect for his parents.

- When entering homes, especially rooms with carpets, it may be the custom to remove one's shoes first. Always remove your shoes before entering a mosque.

- Men and women rarely exhibit any signs of affection in public.

- To beckon someone, put the hand out, palm down, and curl the fingers in and out in a scratching motion.

- The "thumb's up" gesture is considered vulgar.

- To signal "no," move the head up and back sharply. To signal "yes," dip the head downward with a slight twist.

- Avoid blowing your nose in public. Refrain from slouching in a chair or stretching your legs out in front of you. Also, watch where you point the sole of your shoe, which is considered offensive to anyone seeing it.

Israel

- Warm handshakes are the custom here, and good friends will accompany the handshake with friendly pats to the shoulders or back. Israelis do not usually embrace or hug when meeting unless they are very close friends.

- Some Israelis are very expressive with hands and bodies, and others are more reserved and sedate.

- Israelis stand quite close to one another when conversing. It is also common to see them touch a person on the arm while talking. Touching is common between friends.

- An Israeli insult is to point down at the upturned palm of one hand with the forefinger of the other hand, implying that "grass will grow on my hand" before the speaker's comments come true.

- Western-style eating etiquette is practiced throughout Israel.

- All of the popular gestures described in Chapter 2 are known in Israel: the "O.K." sign with thumb and forefinger means just that and is not vulgar; "thumbs up" means "O.K."; the vertical horn means "cuckold"; the "fig" is a sexual comment; the "V" means "victory," and so on.

Kenya

- The most common physical greeting is the conventional handshake as imported by British colonizers. However, members of some local tribes may greet one another by gently slapping palms and then gripping each other's cupped fingers.

- Using the left hand to receive a gift is considered impolite.

- Take care when photographing local residents; it is best to ask permission in advance.

- Many of the gestures and body language from Britain are known and used in Kenya.

Jordan

- Both friends and strangers are greeted warmly, with sincere handshaking. Long acquaintances of the same sex may embrace lightly and kiss either cheek.

- Among the elderly and more traditional, the *salaam* greeting may be used. That is done by taking the right hand, touching the heart, then the forehead and then gesturing forward. The verbal expression is *salaam alaykum,* or "peace be with you."

- Guests are always warmly received.

- When dining, it is the custom to refuse offers of additional food at least two times, then accept on the third offer if you actually wish more.

- It is polite to leave small portions of food on your plate.

- Coffee in the Middle East is often what Westerners consider thick, syrupy, and strong. It is customarily served in small cups, refilling them often. If, as a visitor, you wish to signal "no more refills," just tip the cup back and forth with your fingers.

- As in other Arab countries, it is impolite to point the sole of your shoe toward another person.

- When crossing the legs, it is the custom here to cross them at the ankles or the knees, but not to place one ankle on the other knee.

Lebanon

- The handshake is the customary greeting, often accompanied by a courteous nod of the head. Also, since many cultures in the Middle East are more touch-oriented, a Lebanese male may touch your arm or pat you on the back as a signal of friendship. Close friends may lightly embrace and kiss each other on the cheeks. Men may tip their hat when greeting a woman.

- As in many Middle Eastern countries, personal space is smaller than in most Western countries. Therefore, people of the same sex tend to stand closer together.

- Children are usually taught to refrain from speaking unless spoken to by visitors.

- Posture is considered important in Lebanon, and gestures and bodily expressiveness are freely used.

- While signaling "yes" is done with a nod, to signal "no" a Lebanese may perform a sharp upward motion of the head accompanied by raised eyebrows.

- To beckon someone, the proper gesture is: palm down, fingers curling in and out in something of a scratching motion.

- It is impolite to show the sole of your shoe to others.

- A gesture which signals "no" is raising the hand, palm outward toward the other person.

- A closed fist raised up into the air is regarded as a rude gesture.

- The following is considered an insulting gesture: hand up, palm outward, fingers spread, drop the middle finger, and hold it down with the thumb.

- Licking the little finger and then brushing it across the eyebrow is a signal that someone is homosexual.

- Many Lebanese men carry "worry beads" that resemble a Catholic rosary but have no special religious significance. They are simply stress-relievers; you will see the men fingering and twisting these beads on the street while walking, while seated, during business meetings and on all types of occasions.

Mali

- The handshake is common and often done with the left hand touching the other person's elbow as well. Many other forms of greetings will be found due to the ethnic diversity in Mali.

163

- Men shake hands with women only if women offer their hand first.

- The Northwestern part of Mali is influenced by Islamic customs, so many of the gestures and body language used in the Arab region will apply there.

- Watch your host for clues and direction, but it is customary to remove one's shoes before entering a room.

Morocco

- Greetings are important in Morocco and come in different forms. In the larger cities, good friends will greet by brushing or kissing cheeks. Multiple kissing implies even closer ties and sincerity. In rural areas, handshakes accompanied by touching the heart with the right hand is often the custom.

- When dining, the host may bring water and a basin for guests to wash their hands.

- It is quite acceptable—common, in fact—to eat with the fingers from a common platter of food. But use the right hand only. Follow the actions of the host.

- Common Arab practices prevail here, such as not showing the sole of the shoe, occasional absences by hosts to attend prayers, and so on.

Nigeria

- Because of diverse cultures in Nigeria, it is difficult to generalize about proper greetings. However, those who travel there as tourists or on business will probably find that the local people they deal with know and use Western conventions.

- Nigerians try very hard to please guests. They are congenial and hospitable, and respect the Western regard for punctuality.

- Among one major ethnic group, the Yorubas, an important guest will be greeted by applause.

- Members of the same sex will stand closer together than most Westerners normally do.

- One vulgar gesture that should be avoided is the "hand push," where the hand is held forward at shoulder or head level, with the fingers spread.

- Avoid pointing the sole of the shoe or foot at a person.

- Use only the right hand for eating finger foods.

- The Yorubas will wink at their children if they want them to leave the room.

Saudi Arabia

- Men will greet each other with a light but sincere handshake, sometimes with the left hand touching the forearm, the elbow, or even the shoulder of the other person.

- A Saudi man accompanied by a veiled woman will probably not introduce her.

- Among Saudi males, an embrace and cheek kissing may be added to their greeting.

- As in other parts of the Middle East, among the elderly and more traditional folk, the *salaam* greeting may be observed. This is done by using the right hand to touch the heart and then the forehead in one upward sweep. It is accompanied by saying *salaam alaykum* or "peace be with you."

- Saudis may signal "yes" by swiveling the head from side-to-side. "No" is indicated by tipping the head backward and clicking the tongue.

- Space relationships are smaller by Western standards. People of the same sex will stand closer together than North Americans or Europeans do.

- While walking along a street or in a corridor, a Saudi host may guide a Western male by gently holding his elbow or even taking his hand and continue walking along hand-in-hand. This is a sign of friendship and respect.

- Many upper class Saudis have been educated in the West or have carefully learned Western ways, so they will be well acquainted with Western customs. Therefore you may receive a firm handshake, no touching, larger spaces, and so on.

- Avoid excessive amounts of pointing or signaling with the hands.

- Joint meetings may be encountered—that is, several groups of business visitors may be seated in separate parts of the same room, with the Saudi host moving from one group to the other.

- Your Saudi host may interrupt a meeting or conversation, leave the room and be gone for 15 or 20 minutes. This usually signifies he has gone to conduct his daily prayers.

- Women are not permitted to drive vehicles.

- Eye contact is important. The saying that "the eyes are the windows to the soul" applies here. Many Westerners observe that Middle Eastern men seem to have "languid" eyes and misinterpret this as boredom or disinterest, which is not necessarily true.

- In this area of the world, the left hand is customarily used for bodily hygiene. Therefore, it should *not* be used for eating, handing over gifts or business cards, or other such gestures.

- Crossing the legs in front of non-Westernized Saudis may be taken as a sign of disrespect. The same applies to putting your foot or feet up on a piece of furniture.

- An insulting gesture here would be as follows: hand up, palm down, fingers spread, with the index finger bent down and pointing outward.

- Avoid showing the sole of your shoe to another person—it can be considered an insult since the sole is the lowest and probably dirtiest part of the body.

- Any display of more intimate areas of the body is disliked; this includes bare shoulders, stomach, and calves and thighs.

- The "worry beads" so common throughout the Middle East will be seen often in Saudi Arabia. This is a string of beads resembling a Catholic rosary, but which carries no similar religious meaning. They are fondled strictly for personal relaxation.

- Smoking of cigarettes in public is not common. However, in some Saudi locations the communal water pipe, or *hooka,* may be passed around among those present.

South Africa

- Since this country is an amalgam of Black African tribal, Dutch and English cultures, influences of each can be found. The handshake is still the commonly accepted form of greeting for most visitors.

- Refer to sections in this listing for The Netherlands and for England for gestures commonly known and used there. Many of these will be known and used by the white population in South Africa.

- The raised right-handed fist has become a world-recognized symbol for "Black Power." In 1990, it received international publicity when South African black leader Nelson Mandela toured Europe and North America.

- Visitors to South African international airports report that porters will approach them with both hands held out in a cupped shape. At first glance, it appears they are begging for a tip, but it is reportedly a signal of humbleness or of supplications saying, in effect, "The gift you may give me (for carrying your bags) will mean so much that I must hold it in two hands."

- The continental style of eating prevails among the white population and many of the blacks. Also, cover the mouth when yawning.

Sudan

- In the North, where Arabic customs prevail, greetings consist of a warm but gentle handshake. Good friends of the same sex may embrace. But men should not take the initiative to shake hands with a woman unless she extends her hand first. In fact, men should not publicly touch a woman.

- As in other Arabic-influence countries, the left hand has limited use: it's role is for bodily hygiene. The right hand should be used for greetings, for eating, for handing over business cards or gifts, and for gesturing. Pointing with the finger may be considered rude.

- Avoid showing the bottom of your shoe to another person, which is considered rude.

- The Arabic language is considered by some a dramatic and emotional language, and conversation is often vigorous and enthusiastic.

Tanzania

- Among the Swahili-speaking coastal population, the handshake is the customary greeting. Local men do not normally shake hands publicly with women, but foreign visitors are often excused for doing so.

- Avoid using the left hand when giving or receiving a business card, gift, envelope, or such.

- Otherwise, most European gestures are known.

Zaire

- As in many African nations, the large number of tribal cultures cause a great diversity in social customs. However, in the capital city of Kinshasa the handshake is the appropriate greeting for visitors.

- There is minimal public contact between men and women.

- Dining is an important social custom here, and one is often judged by one's conduct while eating.

- If your host uses the fingers to eat, do the same but use only the right hand.

Zambia

- The handshake is the accepted greeting here, with possibly the added feature of the left hand supporting the right. This demonstrates respect.

- Among local inhabitants, kneeling before the elderly or social superiors may be observed.

- Among some tribes, gentle thumb-squeezing may be practiced, along with clapping.

- People of the opposite sex rarely have physical contact when greeting.

- Direct eye contact between sexes should be kept to a minimum lest it suggest romantic interests.

- Pointing one's finger at something or someone is considered improper.

- Wash hands before and after eating because the right hand is often used to pick up food from a common bowl or dish. Public spitting is considered a sign of disrespect.

Zimbabwe

- The handshake is the safe, accepted, and common form of greeting. Local women and girls may even curtsy.

- An older tradition is to give—or accept—a gift using both hands.

- Often a signal of thanks and politeness is shown by clapping the hands.

- Avoid long, direct eye contact. This is considered somewhat rude, especially in rural areas.

PACIFIC AND ASIA

Australia

- A firm, friendly handshake is the customary greeting here. It's not necessary, though, to offer to shake hands with a woman unless she offers her hand first. Women friends may kiss when greeting each other. When greeting someone at a distance, a wave is customary but yelling is not.

- Be prepared to exchange business cards, but this practice is not as rigid as in, say, Japan or some European countries.

- In business meetings, eye contact is important.

- When addressing audiences, use erect posture and modest gestures.

- Australian men do not consider it good form to show much emotion, so good friends may pat one another on the back, but

169

there is not much physical expressiveness of emotion beyond that. It is considered unmanly.

- Even if you are friends, winking at a woman is considered rude.

- The "thumbs up" gesture is considered a rude and improper gesture, especially when jerked upward.

- Guests of honor usually sit at the right of the host. Eating is done in the so-called "continental style"—that is, with the fork held constantly in the left hand and the knife in the right. When eating soup, move the spoon away from you and not toward you. To indicate you have finished eating, lay the knife and fork in parallel on your plate. While eating, keep your elbows off the table.

- A yawn must always be covered with the hand, accompanied by "Excuse me."

- Like the British, respect is given for queues, or lines of people. Never barge or jump into a line; always go politely to the end and wait your turn.

- Finishing a drink, turning the glass upside down and putting it squarely on the bar is, in some Australian pubs, a signal that you "can whip anyone in the house."

- Sportsmanlike gestures (e.g., being a good winner, or loser; congratulating a good performance) of any kind are liked and appreciated because good sportsmanship is highly respected.

- Australians are known to be warm, friendly, and informal and dislike overly expressive or "gushy" behavior in any form.

- The more popular and common gestures illustrated and explained in Chapter 2 will probably be known and understood in Australia.

Bangladesh

- Bengalis will shake hands with Western men, but a man merely nods when introduced to a woman of either nationality.

- About 15 percent of the population is Hindi, so the *namaste* is the preferred greeting (hands held chest-high in a prayerlike position).

- Use the right hand for eating—never the left hand. This follows the Middle Eastern custom where the left hand is used only for bodily hygiene.

- Eating utensils are common in the better restaurants, but it is also acceptable and common to eat with the fingers.

- Men and women often dine separately.

- Visit the washroom, if you must, before and after a meal but not during.

- It is considered unclean to transfer food from one person's plate to another, even among married couples.

- The "thumbs up" gesture is considered an obscene gesture in Bangladesh.

- Remove your shoes before entering a mosque. If you notice other people washing their feet as well, do the same.

- Don't take photographs without asking permission in advance.

- Since Bangladesh is a highly populated country, while in crowds there might be considerable pushing and shoving. This is not considered impolite, merely a necessity.

Burma

- It is *not* customary to shake hands, but many Burmese business-people may adopt the Western custom of handshaking, so be prepared either way.

- It is not proper in Burma to show physical expressions of affection in public.

- Buddhism is widely practiced here and in that religion the bottom half of the body is considered lowly. The upper half of the body is regarded with greater esteem.

- The head of the image of Buddha should not be touched.

- The feet are considered "unclean" and therefore it is very rude to raise your feet, such as placing them on a table or desktop.

- You may note that people remove their shoes before entering a home, and always before entering any religious building.

China (People's Republic of)

- The Western custom of shaking hands is spreading rapidly and is now probably the customary form of greeting, but often a nod or slight bow is sufficient. Don't be upset, though, if the Chinese do not smile when being introduced; this is rooted more in the Chinese attitude of keeping feelings inside rather than displaying them openly.

- Business cards are often exchanged, and yours should be printed in your own *and* in the Chinese language. Also, it is more respectful to present your card—or a gift or any other article—using *both* hands.

- Hugging and kissing when greeting are *un*common.

- Generally speaking, the Chinese are not a touch-oriented society. This is especially true for visitors. So avoid touching or any prolonged form of body contact.

- Public displays of affection are very rare. On the other hand, you may note people of the same sex walking hand-in-hand, which is simply a gesture of friendship.

- Avoid being physically demonstrative, especially with older or more senior people.

- Posture is important, so don't slouch or put your feet on desks or chairs. Also, avoid using your feet to gesture or move articles around.

- Personal space is much less in China. This means when conversing, the Chinese will stand much closer than Westerners. This often results in Westerners moving backward, with the Chinese following along in something of an unintended *pas de deux*.

- The Chinese are enthusiastic applauders, so don't be surprised if you are greeted with group clapping, even by small children. When a person is applauded in this fashion it is the custom for that person to return the applause.

- A distinctive Chinese (and Japanese) action is to suck air in quickly and audibly through the lips and teeth. This is a common reaction when something surprising or difficult is proposed or requested. If this reaction is given, it would be best to modify your request rather than risk having your Chinese counterpart face the highly embarrassing (for them) situation of having to say "no."

- When walking in public places, direct eye contact and staring is not common in the larger cities, especially in those areas accustomed to foreign visitors. However, in smaller communities, visitors may be the subject of much curiosity and therefore you may notice some stares, especially if you are blond or red-headed.

- Silence can be a virtue in China, so don't be dismayed if there are periods of silence in your dinner or business conversations. It is a sign of politeness and of contemplation. During conversations, be especially careful about interrupting.

- Don't begin eating until the host picks up his or her chopsticks.

- It is the Chinese way to decline gifts or other offerings two or even three times, even when they want to accept, as a matter of etiquette.

- Seating arrangements are important, whether at business meetings or while dining. At meetings, the chief guest is always seated at the "head of the room," facing the door; the host with his or her back to the door. While dining, the guest sits to the left of the host.

- Before taking any photographs of local people, ask their permission.

- If you wish to smoke, offer your cigarettes to those around you. Chinese women rarely smoke, however. If you object to others smoking in your presence, this may pose a difficult situation since segregated smoking areas are uncommon in China. If this is extremely important to you, one gambit is to explain to your host that you are allergic to cigarette smoke.

- The open hand is used for pointing (*not* one finger).

- To beckon someone, the palm faces downward and the fingers are moved in a scratching motion.

- On public streets, spitting and blowing the nose without the benefit of a handkerchief is fairly common, although the government is waging a campaign to reduce this. It is regarded as ridding the body of a waste and is therefore considered an act of personal hygiene.

- Dining revolves around the use of chopsticks. Just watch your host for tips and techniques. Here are some finer points:

    —With wooden chopsticks, you may see the Chinese first rub them together before eating. This is merely a way of removing any possible splinters. But, if you are a guest, it is impolite to do this because it suggests you have been given cheap, rough chopsticks.

    —Even though there will be communal dishes of food, don't take your portions with the ends of the chopsticks you have put in your mouth. Either your host will place food on your plate, or a separate pair of "serving" chopsticks will be near the serving dish.

    —Don't stick your chopsticks upright in your rice. Among some Chinese this is a superstitious act that could bring bad luck. In some areas placing chopsticks in rice in this fashion is done as an offering to the dead.

    —Don't worry if you drop a chopstick on the floor. Some Chinese believe this means you will get an invitation to dinner.

    —Don't suck on your chopsticks.

    —To eat large pieces of food (when a knife is not available for cutting), it is perfectly acceptable to lift the morsel to your mouth with the chopsticks and bite off a piece.

    —When you are finished eating, place your chopsticks in parallel across your dish or bowl.

- The Chinese will hold bowls of food directly under their lower lip and use the chopsticks to push the food into their mouths. When eating long, slippery noodles it is perfectly acceptable to place one end in your mouth and slurp or suck up the remainder.

- Refusing food may be considered impolite. If you don't wish to eat it, just poke it around and move it to the side of your dish.

- Bones are often placed directly on the table alongside your dish.

- Toothpicks are commonly available and used during and after a Chinese meal. Just be certain to cover your mouth with the other hand while poking and picking.

- Offering toasts is common in China and is a relatively simple and uninvolved act: just raise your glass, look at your host and those around him, nod, and drink. You may also say *Kan-pie*, which means "bottoms up," and some Chinese will actually invert the glass "bottom up" to show they have finished the whole drink.

- Don't worry about a bit of pushing and shoving in stores or when groups board public buses or trains. Apologies are neither offered or expected.

- Most of the more popular gestures discussed in Chapter 2 will be familiar to the Chinese. However, many Chinese will not recognize the "O.K." sign; instead, the "thumbs up" signal is known and means "Everything is O.K." When beckoning, the curling inward of the index finger is not used in China.

Fiji

- Fijians greet one another by nodding and then flicking the eyebrows upward. Otherwise, the handshake is the customary greeting with visitors.

- The custom here is to remove your shoes when entering a home.

- Fijians love to laugh, so you will find much joviality here.

- To exhibit respect when speaking to another person, stand with your arms folded behind your back.

- It is considered impolite to touch a Fijian's head. (Yes, it's true that the impulse to touch a Fijian's head may not be the strongest or most common, but just in case. . . .)

- Beckoning is done by extending the hand, palm downward, and scratching toward you.

- When speaking with someone, direct eye contact is good but avoid prolonged staring.

Hong Kong

- After almost a century as a British Crown Colony, many British customs prevail. This includes the straightforward, traditional shaking of hands. If there is any variation, it might be that the grip is less firm than in the United States, and the Chinese may stand closer than Americans or Europeans do.

- When conversing, conspicuous blinking of the eyes is considered impolite. It suggests disrespect and boredom.

- To beckon someone, extend the arm, palm downward, and make a scratching motion with the fingers. Never use the index finger, palm up and toward you, in a back and forth curling motion toward your body. That gesture is used only for animals.

- To signal a waiter that you wish the check or bill, make a writing motion with your two hands.

- The Chinese population here is uncomfortable with any casual or prolonged bodily contact. However, two Chinese of the same sex will be seen on occasion walking along hand-in-hand. This nearly always signifies nothing more than friendship.

- When seated, it is the custom to place the hands in the lap and not wiggle the legs.

- When pointing to something, do so with the open hand and not just one or two fingers.

- When dining, Oriental and Western customs are both common and often intermixed. So be prepared for the use of chopsticks as well as knives and forks. With the latter, the continental style is used, with the fork remaining constantly in the left hand. (See the section on the People's Republic of China for more information on the nuances of using chopsticks.)

- Toasting is common, with the host at a large party often visiting each table to present a toast. One appropriate time to make toasts is when the shark's fin soup is served, a delicacy at Chinese meals and often considered the apex of the meal.

- During business meetings, tea may be served. Don't touch yours until the host begins. If he lets the tea sit untouched for a long period, that may be a signal that the meeting is finished.

- Many of the popular gestures illustrated and described in Chapter 2 will be known in Hong Kong, having been imported by a constant stream of Western, and especially British, visitors.

India

- The traditional greeting in India is the *namaste*, where the palms of the hands are pressed together in a praying position and held about chest high, then accompanied with a slight bow forward. Westerners can use the *namaste* as a greeting, and such a show of knowledge about Indian customs will be appreciated. The *namaste* is also used when saying goodbye.

- Men customarily do not touch women in either formal or informal situations.

- A Western woman should not initiate a handshake with a man. Most Indian women will shake hands with foreign women but not men.

- Indian businessmen may indulge in warm and even enthusiastic back-patting and slapping. This is merely a sign of cordiality and friendship.

- Carry and be prepared to exchange business cards.

- When walking the streets, try not to stare, especially at the impoverished; that is considered a way to humiliate them.

- Near temples and other holy places, street salespeople will approach you, hand outstretched, as if wanting to shake your hand. That is merely a ruse to allow them to fasten a religious bracelet on the arm and then demand a donation.

- Showing anger is usually the worst way to accomplish almost anything.

- When taking photographs of people, be sure to ask permission first.

- Ask permission before you smoke cigarettes, pipes, or cigars.

- Whistling in public is considered very impolite.

- Here, as in many places in Asia, public displays of affection are neither common nor considered proper, even among married couples.

- If an Indian smiles and jerks his head backward, it could signal "yes." However, in the south of India, if a person moves his head quickly back and forth it signals "Yes, I understand what you are saying."

- The head is considered a sacred part of the body. Therefore, don't pat youngsters on the head or touch an older person's head.

- Women should cover their heads when entering a sacred building.

- As in the Middle East, where the feet and soles of the shoes are considered the lowest and dirtiest part of the body, the same is true in India. Therefore, try not to touch anyone or point at anyone with your shoes or their soles.

- A somewhat unique gesture in India is to grasp one's earlobes. It expresses remorse or honesty, as a servant might do when scolded.

- When you wish to point, use your chin, the full hand or maybe the thumb, but *not* a single finger. Pointing with a single finger is used only with inferiors. The chin is not used to point to people who are considered superiors. The best way to signal attention toward something or someone is with the full hand.

- Remove shoes before entering a temple or mosque. Once inside, don't touch paintings or statues.

- The standard way of beckoning another person is with the arm extended, palm down, and with a scratching motion inward with the fingers.

- Beckoning a waiter is done in different ways: locals may snap their fingers and hiss; Westerners should do it the Western way, but don't use the one-curled-finger method.

- Whereas Europeans might wave "good-bye" by using the hand and arm in an up-and-down motion this will probably be interpreted in India as signaling "come here."

- When dining, be certain to wash your hands before and after the meal. If utensils are not offered, the fingertips and full hand (right hand only) are used. Transfer food from the communal dish to your plate with a spoon, not with your fingers.

- Hosts will often serve you, and to refuse food could be an insult. If you have objections to any foods, inform your hosts in advance. Use the *namaste* to respectfully signal that you have had enough food.

- The left hand should be used sparingly; pass gifts or other articles with the right hand, eat with the right hand, and point with the right hand.

- A few of the popular gestures described and illustrated in Chapter 2 will be known in India, having been imported over the decades by many visitors. It is wise to use them sparingly, however, and before you do, ask local friends about their local interpretation.

Indonesia

- When meeting for the first time, the handshake, accompanied by a slight nod of the head, is the customary greeting for both men and women. After that, it is not as common—maybe when congratulating someone, or when saying goodbye.

- Men rarely touch women in public except to shake hands.

- Foreign visitors should refrain from kissing in public. This is not only improper but it could even generate anger.

- If you cross your legs when seated, cross them at the knees or the ankles but not with one ankle propped on the other knee.

- If you are seated and your host or hostess enters the room, be sure to rise.

- Indonesians hate to disappoint people, so they will rarely disagree in public and they will laugh to mask anger, shock or embarrassment. It is also impolite to laugh at someone else's mistake or misfortune.

- In tourist areas, street salespeople will crowd closely and even touch you in order to get your attention.

- Indonesians respond to praise with a smile and a nod, but no more. They are uncomfortable with excessive acts of gratitude and also with loud voices and any outward bursts of anger.

- Eating while walking on the street is inappropriate.

- Yawning in public is somewhat impolite, but if necessary should be accompanied by covering the mouth.

- Watch your host, but it may be the custom where you are visiting to remove your shoes before entering certain places, like carpeted rooms, feasting places, funerals, and holy places.

- Remove sunglasses when speaking to someone or entering a home.

- People in Bali may be seen topless and washing and bathing in streams and rivers while in the nude. Do not take photographs.

- Eat only with the right hand and avoid showing the sole of your shoe in the presence of other people.

- Beckoning someone is done by extending the arm, palm downward, and then doing a scratching motion toward your body.

- It is generally considered impolite to put your hands in your pockets while standing and conversing with another person.

- You can pat another person on the shoulder to express approval, but avoid touching the head.

- To point, Indonesians will extend the thumb instead of the forefinger.

- Using the head for gestures or to make faces is impolite, as is tossing an object or article to another person.

- Fingers can be used for eating, but utensils are also used. When at the dining table, keep both hands on the table. Avoid using toothpicks in public.

- In crowded restaurants, it is not uncommon for others to ask if they may sit at your table.

- To beckon a waiter, just raise your hand. To call for the bill, make a writing motion with both hands.

- If you are a guest, wait for your host to invite you to begin eating. Then, during the dinner, don't be concerned if the conversation is sparse; it is the custom here to concentrate on the food.

- When you finish eating, leave just a little food on your plate. If you clean the plate, it is a signal that you would like more food.

- On public buses, it is customary for men to give up their seats to women and for men and women to offer their seats to the elderly.

Japan

- As most visitors already know, the graceful act of bowing is the traditional greeting for the Japanese. However, the Japanese have also adopted the Western practice of shaking hands, albeit with a light grip and perhaps with eyes averted. The reasons are that a firm grip to them suggests aggression, and direct eye contact is considered slightly intimidating. It should be added, however, that many well-traveled Japanese are carefully study-ing Western ways and therefore may surprise you with a *firm* grip and *direct* eye contact.

- Meanwhile, to show respect for their customs, it would flatter them to offer a slight bow when being introduced. (For addi-tional comments on the art of bowing, see pages 24–28.)

- The seemingly simple act of exchanging business cards is more complex in Japan because the business card represents not only one's identity but one's station in life. Here are some tips on what you may encounter:

  —The business card is held with both hands, grasped between the thumbs and forefingers.

  —It is extended forward in a respectful gesture with the print-ing pointed considerately toward the other person. A slight bow is made at the same time.

  —The Japanese will take the card, again with both hands and a reciprocal bow, and then read the card carefully. This may be followed by another slight bow.

  —After this sequence, the Western handshake may occur. (Or, in deference to the Westerner, the greeting may begin with handshaking and then evolve to bowing and the above ritual of exchanging business cards.)

  —When Westerners take the business card from a Japanese, they should avoid examining it casually and quickly tucking it into a coat or shirt pocket. Examine it carefully, then place it on the table in front of you for further reference.

  —Avoid scribbling notes on the back of the card. This shows a certain measure of disrespect for something that represents a person's identity.

- Avoid clapping a Japanese on the back, standing very close, any form of public kissing, or any prolonged physical contact. On crowded public transportation, however, it is a different matter. People are accustomed to being jammed into tight spaces, as epitomized by the transit employees whose jobs consist of pack-ing people into the public trains before the doors close.

- When in meetings, periods of silence may occur. This is perfectly acceptable and customary. During these periods, the Japanese may even raise their eyes to look over the heads of others while contemplating.

- Queues are generally respected; it is only in crowded train and subway stations where the huge volume of people causes touching and pushing.

- Because of the high regard for graciousness and restraint, one should not shout, raise the voice in anger, or exhibit any excessively demonstrative behavior.

- Among the Japanese, smiling often can cover a gamut of emotions: happiness, anger, confusion, apologies, or sadness.

- Displaying an open mouth is considered rude in Japan. That is one reason many Japanese, especially the women, cover their mouths when giggling or laughing.

- The Japanese have great difficulty voicing an outright "no" to a question or statement. But, waving the hand back and forth in front of one's own face (palm outward) is one way of saying "I don't know" or "I don't understand"—but it is also done in the context of humility, as when receiving a compliment, signaling "No, I am undeserving."

- Correct posture is important in Japan, especially when seated. Consequently, avoid slouching or putting your feet on a table or stool. Balance in life is a basic Japanese principle, so a square, solid posture when seated or walking is practiced (for example, both feet squarely on the ground, arms in the lap or on the armrests). Any slouching or leaning back in a tipped chair can be interpreted as showing an "I don't care" attitude.

- Listening is considered not only polite in Japan, but also is regarded as a valuable business skill. Americans and other Westerners tend to interrupt. In fact, author John C. Condon writes that the three top complaints the Japanese have about Americans is: They talk too much, they interrupt, and then don't listen.

- Crossing the legs at the knees or ankles is the preferred form rather than with one ankle over the other knee.

- To get the attention of a waiter, catch his eye, and dip your head downward.

- To beckon someone, put your arm out, palm down, and make a scratching motion with the fingers.

- It is considered insulting to point to someone with four fingers extended and the thumb folded into the palm.

- When the hand and fingers are used to count, the Japanese use the thumb to represent the number "five." Therefore the "thumb's up" gesture in Japan can signify the number "five."

- The "O.K." gesture in Japan may be interpreted as the signal for "money," probably because the circular shape formed by the index finger and thumb suggests the shape of a coin. For example, a Japanese may make a purchase at a food counter and then flash this gesture to signal "Give me my change in coins."

- When a Japanese is speaking in his own language, he may gesture with one hand, fingers slightly pursed, and point the hand slightly at himself—toward his face. This is simply an emphatic way of saying "I" or "me" or "myself."

- In many restaurants, it is the custom for men to sit cross-legged on the floor. Women should sit either on their legs or have them tucked to one side. For Westerners who find this uncomfortable, Japanese restaurants often provide a small armrest, allowing you to sit with legs folded on one side while leaning your weight on the armrest.

- Bathing in Japanese baths is a new experience for most visitors because it is usually done in stages. It can involve soaking in one tub, exiting to soap and lather up, rinsing and then entering a new tub. Avoid soaping up, rinsing and soaking all in one tub.

- Blowing your nose in public is considered rude. In Japan, the handkerchief is used primarily for wiping the mouth or drying the hands when leaving the washroom. Paper tissues are used for blowing the nose and then discarded.

- Many Japanese will be seen in public wearing white gauze masks, like those used in a hospital surgery room. This is not because they fear air pollution, but instead because they probably have a cold and do not wish to pass along the germs to others.

- Present a gift with both hands, as with business cards. This is viewed as a gesture of humility, and humility is important in Japan. It is a nice touch to bow slightly while doing either act. Also, when receiving a gift, you are not expected to open it right then and there. Wait until later, in private.

- Avoid standing with your hand or hands in your pockets, especially when greeting someone or when addressing a group of people.

- If you are eating with chopsticks, follow some of the customs outlined in the earlier section on China (see page 174). However, the Japanese hold bowls of food lower and not right under the chin.

- When eating, pick up dishes on your left side with your right hand and vice versa.

- Toasting is quite common in Japan. It is a simple action of raising the glass and saying one word: *Kan-pie*, which literally means "drain the cup," or as Westerners might say, "Bottoms up."

- At public restaurants or private homes, it is often the custom to remove your shoes before entering. You'll either see a line-up of other shoes from other restaurant patrons at the doorstep, or just follow the actions of your host. Shoes are usually placed with the toes pointing toward the exit.

- A formal Japanese tea ceremony is just that—a ceremony. It is graceful, expressive, and artistic. Watch your host for the proper procedure.

- In summary, for most visitors the Japanese customs are complex and difficult to understand. Remember two things: (1) style, or the *way* things are done, is just as important as substance, or *what* is being done; and (2) watch your Japanese hosts carefully and follow their example.

Korea, South

- Among themselves, bowing is the traditional form for both greeting and departing. Western and Korean male friends usually greet with both a slight bow and shaking hands. When shaking hands, both hands are sometimes used. Women usually do not shake hands, especially with men, but usually just nod slightly.

- The senior person offers to shake hands first, but the junior person bows first.

- Business cards are traded respectfully. Keep the card on the table in front of you as just one small gesture of respect.

- Good eye contact is important during conversations but not an absolute requirement.

- Two men may be seen walking along holding hands, and it is merely a sign of friendship, nothing more. But in almost all other situations, avoid touching, gripping, or patting a Korean on the arm, shoulder, or back unless you are *very* good friends.

- In public situations, however, personal space is very limited and Western visitors may be disconcerted by the closeness of others in markets, on buses, or while walking on the sidewalks.

- Men generally have priority in Korea: go through a door first, walk ahead of women, and women may help them on with their coats.

- When saying goodbye, the traditional gesture is the bow, but the younger generation has adopted the Western custom of waving goodbye by moving the arm side-to-side.

- The Western version of gesturing "come here"—arm and hand up, palm toward the face—is used only for calling dogs. The correct way to beckon someone in Korea is to extend the arm, palm down, and make a scratching motion.

- When you are standing and having a conversation with someone, a Korean may pass between the two of you instead of walking around. The polite thing is to step backward to allow the person through. The reason for this is that in Korea it is impolite to make someone walk behind your back.

- When walking in public, the convention in Korea is to keep to the left side of the walkway.

- Avoid putting your foot or feet up on a table or chair, or slouching when seated.

- Koreans, especially women, will cover their mouths when laughing. This results in giggling rather than wide-open-mouth laughing.

- Shoes are removed before entering a Korean home.

- Koreans, like other Orientals, like to avoid saying "no," but one gesture that is often used to signal "no" or that "something is very difficult" is to tip the head backward and audibly suck air in through the teeth.

- Loud talking or laughing is usually avoided, unless the occasion is business entertainment. Then, after dinner, there may be solo and group singing and much laughter.

- Older people receive much respect in Korea, so it is appropriate to rise when a person—especially an elderly man enters the room.

185

- Laughter is used to disguise many emotions: Anger, frustration, and even fear.

- Avoid eating food while walking along a public street.

- When dining, chopsticks will probably be used. Follow the same general instructions given earlier in the section on China. (See page 174.)

- When dining, the elderly are served first and the children last.

- During a dinner, a small communal cup may be passed along; drink from it and pass it on. It is also polite for you to fill your neighbor's small soy sauce dish and vice versa.

- Avoid pouring your own drink. It is usually done for you, and you should offer to pour for others. Lift up your glass when receiving a drink, and when you pour for others support your forearm with the other hand. (If all this sounds a bit complicated, just watch how the Koreans around you do it.)

- Drunkenness is quickly forgiven in Korea unless it is accompanied by either gross or aggressive behavior.

- After a Korean dinner, if there is group or solo singing, try to go along with the fun. If asked to sing solo, the polite response is to sing—no matter how simple the song or how poorly you sing.

- At a restaurant, one person usually pays for all, and there may be good-natured argument over the right to pay. Usually, the younger person pays for the elder.

- Lines in public are not necessarily respected, so don't be upset by a bit of pushing and shoving.

- Blowing the nose in public is considered rude. Also, dispose of tissues rather than returning them to a pocket or purse.

- Don't open a gift the moment it is received; instead, wait until later, in private.

- Food and other objects are passed using the right hand, often with the left hand supporting the right forearm.

- As in other Oriental countries, proper posture is important. Stand or sit erectly or squarely. If you must cross your legs, do so at the knees. Try to keep your hands in sight of the person one is talking with.

- If you are wearing sunglasses, remove them during any conversation with another person.

- Toothpicks may be offered at the end of a meal and it is acceptable to use them in front of others, but be certain to cover your mouth with the other hand.

- Periods of silence are common and accepted, even during dinners. Don't be disturbed if there are gaps in the conversation.

- It is considered impolite to enter a room without knocking first. However, Koreans may not wait for you to come to the door and open it. They may knock and then enter. This also applies in public toilets where locks may not function. In these cases, if you are occupying a public toilet stall, just clear your throat or knock back to signal that your stall is in use.

- Bathroom doors are usually kept closed, so knock or make a slight cough first to determine if the bathroom is in use.

- When you enter a conference or dining room, wait to be directed to the seat designated for you. Even if you are the guest of honor, do not proceed directly to the chair of honor. In fact, you may even make slight protestations about accepting the highest seat. This demonstrates humility and is appreciated by Koreans.

- Many of the gestures described and illustrated in Chapter 2, will be known in Korea, mainly because they have been imported by Westerners. But use them with caution, and if at all possible ask Korean friends about them.

Malaysia

- There are three distinct cultures here: Malay (53%), Chinese (32%), and Indian (15%)—each with its own customs. Among all three, shaking hands is the customary greeting, but watch for these differences:

  —Chinese of different sexes will shake hands, but not the Malays or Indians, and if a Chinese woman wishes to shake hands she will make the first move. Chinese men will also often greet one another with a friendly pat on the arm. The Chinese are uncomfortable with any hugging or kissing, unless you are unusually good friends.

  —Malays will often bow slightly when greeting others. This may be accompanied by the *salaam* gesture of greeting: offering one or both hands and lightly touching the hands of the other person; then bringing the hand(s) to the heart, signifying "I greet you from my heart." Both hands are used

187

when greeting older or more senior people as a sign of respect.

—Indians may greet you with the *namaste,* placing the hands in a prayerlike position, chest high, and bowing slightly.

- The Chinese are extremely hospitable and will never reveal if you have committed an error in behavior. So, watch for little signals—a quizzical expression, an upturned eye—and then subtly inquire of a friend if you have inadvertently erred.

- Give respect to elderly people: open doors for them, give up your seat to them, and don't smoke without asking their permission first.

- Smiling or laughing at someone else's discomfort or misfortune is used to cover up embarrassment.

- Among the Malays and Indians, avoid touching someone else's head. That is where they believe the spirit or soul resides. In fact, people of the opposite sex should avoid any kind of casual touching of one another.

- Since showing the sole of the shoe is considered rude, try to keep your feet planted firmly on the ground. Also, don't use your feet for pointing or for moving objects.

- When a person stands with hands on hips, it is a sign of anger.

- Smacking your closed fist into the palm of the other hand is considered a rude gesture.

- Among the Malays, avoid pointing with your forefinger. Instead, point with the thumb, with the other four fingers curled into the palm.

- Older Malays will take offense at the "hang loose" gesture (thumb and little finger protruding) because for them it means "God is bad."

- To beckon someone, never use the index finger in a curling motion. Instead, extend the arm, palm down, and make a scratching motion toward you with your fingers.

- Always cover your mouth when yawning.

- Among the Malays and Indians, the rule while dining is to use only the right hand. The left hand is used for bodily hygiene and is therefore considered "unclean," and should not be used for touching others or passing along gifts or other objects.

- Remove your shoes before entering mosques.

- In homes and certain public buildings, if you are seated on the floor, men sit crosslegged while women customarily sit with their legs tucked under them.

- To get a waiter's attention, just raise your hand. Avoid hissing, shouting, or pointing with one finger.

- At the dinner table, it is considered rude to blow your nose or clear your throat in front of others. Go to the washroom and do these actions in private.

- Malays eat with their right hand only and spoons. You may use a fork in the left hand to push food into the spoon that is held in the right hand.

- Indians eat with the fingers of the right hand, while guests will usually be provided with a fork and spoon. Indians never soil the fingers above the first knuckle and never suck or lick the fingers to clean them.

- The Chinese eat with chopsticks and spoons—the spoons are used for soups and other liquid foods. Using the left hand to eat is perfectly acceptable among the Chinese.

- Some superstitions among the Chinese while eating: placing your chopsticks across your plate signals that you are still hungry; instead, place them on the little "resting stand"; never stick a chopstick upright in a bowl of rice because this is a symbol used at a Chinese funeral; waving chopsticks in the air to gesture is bad manners; slurping soup and belching during a meal are both acceptable. (See page 174 for additional guidelines for eating with chopsticks.)

- Among the Malays, when toasting or handing a dish to another person, it shows respect if you do as follows: use the right hand, but allow the left hand to support the right at the wrist or forearm.

- Malayans don't queue, or form a line, for public buses.

- If you see a prayer rug in a Muslim's office or home, be certain not to stand on it or touch it with your feet.

- Indians have a unique way of indicating agreement: They move their head quickly from side to side. Many Westerners misread this gesture as meaning "no."

- Indians never use the left hand for social purposes—ever!

- As a final note, because of these mixed cultures and the slight differences between them, the best guideline is to observe your host and others around you and follow their example.

New Zealand

- The conventional handshake with firm grip and direct eye contact is the custom here. Men should wait for a woman to offer her hand first.

- The original inhabitants were the Polynesian Maori and, while they are a minority now, their culture still thrives. The traditional greeting among Maori tribespeople is to rub noses.

- The large majority of the population is of British descent, therefore, many British customs for body language and gestures prevail.

- Loud speech and excessive demonstrative behavior is frowned upon.

- Chewing gum and using toothpicks in public are considered bad manners.

- New Zealanders eat in the continental style, meaning fork constantly in the left hand, knife in the right.

- Be sure to cover the mouth when yawning.

- Ask permission before photographing anyone, especially the Maori.

- Most of the more popular gestures described in Chapter 2 will be known in New Zealand with special attention to the "V for victory" sign—as in England, if done with the palm *inward* it is a very rude gesture.

Okinawa

- The traditional greeting here is the bow, both when meeting and when departing. However, because of the strong and long Western influence, handshaking is also common.

- Many of the practices concerning closeness, touching, and open displays of affection that are found in Japan are also prevalent here.

- When entering a private home, it is usually customary to remove your shoes and place them with the toes pointing toward the outdoors.

- The following body actions are important:

  —Avoid yawning in public situations.

  —Posture is important, so don't slouch when sitting and try to maintain a balanced posture at all times.

  —If you cross your legs, do so at the knees and not with one ankle on top of the other knee.

  —Laughter not only signals pleasure but it is also used to mask embarrassment.

  —Avoid eating on the street.

- Chopsticks are used when dining, although Western utensils are freely available. (See the section on China, page 174, for complete guidelines on proper use of chopsticks.)

Pakistan

- The handshake is the common greeting, although with a more gentle grip than Westerners may use. Close friends of the same sex may embrace. A Western man should refrain from touching or shaking hands with a Pakistani woman unless she offers her hand. Western women, however, may extend a hand to be shaken by a Pakistani man.

- It is the custom to be greeted with an offer of coffee, tea, or other refreshment. The custom is always to accept, otherwise you may risk offending your host.

- Since this is a Muslim country, many of the gestures and body language found in the Middle East will apply here. These include such things as:

—Eat only with the right hand because the left hand is used for bodily hygiene and is considered unclean.

—Women are often kept separated in social situations.

—Women dress and act modestly in all settings.

—Two men may be seen walking along holding hands. This is nothing more than a sign of friendship.

—The Muslim practice of praying five times each day is strictly observed here, so don't object or interrupt if someone is praying.

—Avoid trying to photograph Pakistani women, at least without asking permission beforehand.

—The sole of the shoe is considered lowly and dirty, so avoid pointing or showing it to another person.

- In public setting, Pakistani men may be what Western women would consider as forward. Intentional bumping or touching may occur; Western women should avoid any actions such as casual physical or eye contact that could be interpreted as encouragement.

- Staring is common in the Pakistani culture. Don't be offended if you find yourself the object of a steady gaze.

- One obscene gesture in Pakistan is the *closed fist.*

- Remove your shoes before entering a mosque. Avoid walking in front of someone who is praying. Speak in whispers. Don't touch any objects, and don't smoke.

- Dining is done with Western utensils. Use the fork in the left hand to push food into the spoon, held in the right hand.

- Public buses are notoriously crowded, with much touching, pushing and shoving.

Philippines

- Handshaking is the common custom, with both men and women shaking hands in a friendly and informal fashion. With children, it is best to let them initiate the greeting as a sign that they know how to be respectful. A Filipino child may even take a visitor's hand and press it against his own forehead as a gesture of respect.

- Filipinos may greet one another with the "eyebrow flash" which is merely a quick lifting of the eyebrows.

- People of the same sex may be seen holding hands in public, but this usually represents nothing more than friendship.

- Staring at someone is considered rude.

- Respect is always shown to elderly people.

- Speaking in a loud voice is considered ill-mannered and rude.

- As in other parts of the Far East, laughter is used to convey both enjoyment and pleasure but also to mask embarrassment over another person's misfortune.

- Over-imbibing alcohol is considered rude, and being rude is generally a stronger taboo in the Philippines than elsewhere.

- Before taking photographs, always request the permission of your subjects first.

- Filipino women rarely, if ever, smoke in public.

- Instead of pointing to an object, Filipinos will shift their eyes toward it, or purse the lips and point with the mouth.

- If you stand with your hands on your hips, it will be interpreted by Filipinos as a sign that you are angry or challenging another person.

- To beckon someone, never curl your index finger back and forth because that is considered insulting. The proper way to beckon is to extend the arm, palm down, and move the fingers in a scratching motion. The best way to call a waiter is to simply raise the hand, with fingers held closely together.

- Dining is done with Western utensils, but the fork is often held in the left hand and used to push food into the spoon, which is held in the right hand.

- Try to leave a bit of food on your plate to signal to your host that they have provided enough food.

- During business entertaining, as in South Korea, you may be asked to participate in single or group singing. Try to go along with the fun.

- When using public transportation, Filipinos seldom queue or observe orderly lines.

- Because of the long American presence in these islands, Filipinos will recognize most of the popular gestures shown in Chapter 2.

Samoa

- Greetings are usually rather formal and flowery in speech. Samoans enjoy eloquent speech. Visitors are expected to reply in kind.

- When visiting a Samoan home, don't enter until the mats have been spread on the floor. Then leave your shoes at the door. When seated on these mats, sit crosslegged.

- Conversation is conducted while seated.

- Avoid stretching your legs out in front of you because pointing your feet at your host or toward the middle of the home is impolite. If you must stretch your legs, cover them with a mat.

- Don't eat while standing inside a home, or while walking in the roads and streets.

- The national beverage is *kava;* when it is offered to you it is customary to spill a few drops before drinking.

Singapore

- Because of the strong and long British influence, the Island of Singapore follows many British traditions. Therefore, a handshake is the conventional form of greeting, and if the person is Oriental it might be accompanied with a slight bow. When introduced to a woman, it is best to let her make the first move toward handshaking.

- The elderly receive great respect: holding doors for them, rising when they enter the room, and giving up your seat for them on public transportation.

- Some improprieties among non-British ethnic groups:

  —Don't touch someone on top of their head; among many non-British residents, it is believed this is where the spirit resides.

—When crossing the legs, do so at the knees so that the sole of your shoe is not displayed to other people.

—Since the foot is considered the lowliest and dirtiest part of the body, do not use your feet to touch or move other objects.

—Avoid beckoning someone by curling the index finger back and forth. The proper way to beckon someone is to extend the arm, palm down, and wiggle the fingers in a scratching motion.

• Littering in public is absolutely forbidden and, if a person is caught, he can be subjected to heavy fines. This even includes discarded cigarettes.

• Keep in mind that Singapore's residents include many Malaysians (Malays, Chinese, Indians), so be certain to be familiar with the list of gestures for Malaysia as well.

Sri Lanka

• The culture here is strongly influenced by British traditions, so handshaking British-style will be common. However, there are also many different ethnic groups and castes and each of these will have its own nuances when people greet one another.

• Aside from the handshake, the other traditional greeting is the *namaste*. Westerners are not expected to initiate this form of greeting, but it would show politeness and respect to perform this in return.

• Sri Lankan women will be comfortable shaking hands with any Westerner. Western men should, however, avoid embracing Sri Lankan women when greeting.

• Extinguish a cigarette before meeting someone.

• Sri Lankans often smile instead of saying "thank you." However, Western women should be cautious about smiling too much in public. A smile is also considered a form of flirtation.

195

- A caste system still exists here, so if you invite someone to sit down and they are reluctant, don't keep insisting.

- Nodding the head up and down signifies "no," while shaking it back and forth indicates "yes." This is just the opposite from the Western custom so watch for it carefully and whenever the least bit confused be certain to ask for a verbal answer.

- As in many Middle Eastern and Asian countries, the left hand is used for bodily hygiene and so is considered "the unclean hand." Therefore, eat only with your right hand, and when passing objects from one person to another use only your right hand.

- Remove shoes and hat when entering a mosque.

- Any image of Buddha is considered sacred, so don't touch one and *never* lean or sit on one.

Tahiti

- Shake hands when introduced in Tahiti. In fact, it is the custom to carefully shake hands with everyone present. If you don't, it is considered impolite. Because of the strong French influence throughout these islands, Tahitian friends will often greet one another by kissing cheeks.

- Remove your shoes before entering a Tahitian home.

- Wash your hands before eating because Tahitians usually eat with their hands.

Taiwan (The Republic of China)

- Taiwanese are very accustomed to Western visitors so the handshake has become a common and accepted greeting. However, a nod of the head is also sufficient.

- Business cards should be exchanged, and take the time to read the other person's card carefully; place it near you for reference rather than quickly putting it aside or in your pocket.

- Avoid touching a child on the top of his or her head.

- Remove shoes before entering a home.

- Great respect is afforded the elderly, so it is important to let your actions reflect this. Speak to them first. Hold doors open for them. Rise when they enter a room. Give up your seat if no others are available. Remove glasses when addressing them.

- One gesture of special respect for the elderly is to cover your left fist with your right hand and raise both hands to your heart.

- Loud, boisterous, or rude behavior is a strong taboo in Taiwan.

- Youthful friends of the same sex may be seen holding hands, but avoid putting your arm around the shoulders of any Taiwanese.

- A balanced posture is considered important, so Taiwanese men will usually sit with both feet firmly fixed to the floor. Women may cross their legs at the knees or ankles.

- Don't use your feet to move or touch other objects because the feet are considered lowly and dirty.

- The gesture to indicate "no" is to lift your hand to face level, palm facing outward, and moving it back and forth like a windshield wiper.

- To point, don't use the index finger; use the whole hand instead.

- To beckon someone, extend the arm, palm downward, and make a scratching motion with the fingers. Never beckon someone using the forefinger in a curling motion, back and forth.

- When dining, chopsticks are the normal utensils, although in restaurants that cater to Westerners knives and forks will be available. For tips and guidelines on using chopsticks, refer to the section on China (page 174).

- Toasting, both before and during dinner, is common in Taiwan. The toasting word is *Kan-pie,* which means "bottoms up."

- Always present and receive gifts with *both* hands.

Thailand

- The traditional greeting in Thailand is called the *wai,* where the hands are placed together in a prayerlike position and the head is nodded in a slight bow. It is almost identical to the *namaste* of India. This signifies "hello," "thank you," "goodbye," or even "I'm sorry." When performing the *wai,* the higher the hands the more respect you are conveying, but do not raise the fingertips higher than the face.

- The custom is to remove shoes before entering a home, but some Thais will insist that Westerners keep them on in deference to Western tradition.

- Avoid stepping on doorsills when entering a dwelling. Thais believe a deity resides in the doorsill and stepping there will offend that deity.

- Guests are almost always offered a cold or hot drink and the polite gesture is to accept.

- When dining, a spoon and fork are used—the fork for pushing food into the spoon.

- The most sacred part of the human body is the head. Consequently, avoid touching the top of any person's head. This is often difficult for Westerners who seem to unconsciously pat the heads of young children.

- Conversely, the lowliest parts of the body are the feet and therefore you should not point your toe or heel or any part of the foot at any person or object. Don't use your feet to move objects, and try to avoid showing the sole of your shoe to anyone because that is regarded as impolite.

- Two Western customs—placing your arm over the back of a chair in which another person is sitting, and affectionately patting someone else's shoulders or back—are both considered improper, even offensive.

- Two Thai men may be seen walking along the street and holding hands. This is merely a sign of friendship. Other gestures of affection are rarely displayed in public places.

- As in many countries in the Orient, the smile is used not only to express pleasure and amusement but also to cover up embarrassments of any kind.

- Avoid loud talk, excessive and demonstrative gestures, or any form of anger or boisterous behavior.

- While it may happen only rarely, resist any inclination to throw an object to another person. This is considered rude and impolite in Thailand.

- Pointing with one finger is considered rude and is only done when pointing to objects or animals, never humans. Use your chin or incline your head instead.

- To beckon someone, extend the arm, palm down, and make a scratching motion with the fingers. Don't snap your fingers, hiss or holler.

- Since the left hand is regarded as "unclean," don't eat with it or pass any object to another person using the left hand.

- It is impolite to stand and converse with someone while placing one or both hands in your pockets.

- Remove your shoes before entering a mosque, and give the greatest respect to images of Buddha and pictures of the King.

- Showing anger is one of the worst things you can do during business negotiations.

- When passing in front of someone, especially a more senior or elderly person, lower the upper body slightly.

CENTRAL AND SOUTH AMERICA

Argentina

- A warm handshake is the custom here. As men become well acquainted, the handshake might be accompanied by a light touch on the forearm or elbow. Good friends will greet with an *abrazo*, or embrace. This may also include several hearty pats on the back.

- Women friends kiss each other on the cheek and shake hands with both hands, but will not usually talk to strangers without first being properly introduced.

- Men and women who are long-time acquaintances may also exchange a light hug and a "pretended kiss" on the cheek. This means merely brushing cheeks together and making a soft sound as if kissing.

- Women friends may be seen walking along the street arm-in-arm.

- When conversing, Argentines may stand closer than North Americans or Europeans do. Also, an Argentine man may even touch the arm or shoulder, or even finger the lapel of the man he is speaking with.

- Good eye contact is important. Avoid using overly demonstrative gestures.
- Men usually cross their legs knee-over-knee, but this may be considered "unladylike" for women.
- Gestures to avoid in Argentina:
  —Standing with the hands on the hips suggests anger, or a challenge.
  —Yawning in public is rude.
  —Slapping the inside of the thighs near the groin is considered an obscene male gesture.
  —Never pour wine by grasping the neck of the bottle with the hand and rotating the hand backward so that the palm turns upward. Also, always pour with the right hand, never the left.
- Argentines have strong national pride over their excellent red wines; if and when toasts are made, the proper gesture is simply to raise your glass to those around you and say "*salud*" (which means "health"), then sip.
- To beckon someone, extend the arm, palm down, and make a scratching motion with the fingers.
- Since there is a strong Italian heritage in Argentina, many gestures from that country are known and used. For example:
  —Brushing the backs of the fingers under the chin and then outward means "I don't know," or "I don't care."
  —The "hook 'em horns" gesture can be interpreted as "Your spouse is cheating on you."
- To signal across a distance to another person that "You have a phone call," Argentines will often point the index finger toward the side of the head and make a circular motion. This can be confusing, because in North America and other regions that gesture can also mean "You are crazy."
- To indicate that something is just "so-so," Argentines will extend the hand and fingers and waggle the thumb up and down: thumb up, then thumb down, repeating it several times.
- Since one of Argentina's most popular sports is soccer, a popular gesture conveying exuberance and victory is to raise the fist upward emphatically, with the knuckles of the fingers pointing outward.

- When dining, many Argentines will cut their meat by placing the fork upright in the meat and putting the knife through the tines for easier cutting.

- To indicate you have finished eating, cross the knife and fork (tines down) in the middle of your plate.

- Some of the popular gestures depicted in Chapter 2 have been imported into Argentina, so they will be known and recognized there. One of those gestures—the "O.K." sign—is a *rude* gesture in the neighboring country of Brazil, so most Argentines will be aware of that gesture and that meaning.

Bolivia

- A warm handshake is the customary greeting. Good male friends will also perform an *abrazo* or embrace accompanied by a few hearty pats on the back, and then maybe even another hand-shake. Female friends will also embrace and touch cheeks in a kissing motion.

- If a person believes his hand is dirty or soiled in any way, he may offer his forearm to shake.

- When two men are standing and conversing, North Americans and Europeans may find themselves feeling uncomfortable be-cause Bolivians (and most Latin Americans) seem to stand so close. There is no hidden symbolism or message here, it's merely that "personal space" is less or narrower.

- When conversing, good eye contact is important. To not do so is considered impolite.

- The "fig" gesture, hand forming a fist with the thumb protrud-ing between index and middle finger, is considered a rude ges-ture in Bolivia.

- In a marketplace, if a vendor holds his hand out, fingers ex-tended and flips the thumb back and forth it merely means "There isn't any left; I don't have any more."

- When yawning, always cover the mouth.

- To beckon someone, extend the arm, palm downward, and move the fingers in a scratching motion.

- When dining, never eat with the fingers. This even pertains to eating chicken. A special fork is often provided for eating fruit.

- At the dinner table, don't put your hands in your lap. Keep them above the table, perhaps resting the wrists lightly on the edge of the table.

- When pouring wine, it is considered extremely rude to pour it with the left hand or "backhanded"—that is, turning the hand over so that the palm faces upward.

Brazil

- A good, warm handshake is the traditional greeting in Brazil. However, because the Brazilians show affection easily, among male friends the *abraço* (Portuguese spelling), or embrace, will be added.

- Women friends will add a light kiss on the cheek, with married women kissing both cheeks. If one or both women is single, a third kiss is added signifying a wish for marriage for the single person(s).

- If a Brazilian woman believes she knows a Western man well enough, during the initial handshake she will draw the man gently forward and offer her cheek to be kissed. Bear in mind this is a "pretended" kiss, with the cheeks just brushing plus a kissing motion.

- People in Brazil will also shake hands when arriving and departing. There may also be a touching of the forearm or elbow, and often a pat on the back.

- If you are conducting business, be certain to bring a plentiful supply of business cards because these are always exchanged. Also, during business meetings expect to be served (often) small cups of very strong coffee.

- Since this is more of a touching society, people stand close together when conversing or when standing in lines.

- If you see an acquaintance at a distance, it is fine to wave but avoid shouting a greeting.

- Don't eat or chew gum while walking on the street.

- Brazilians use hand and body gestures often, and therefore they have a variety of unique motions and meanings. Here are some of the more important ones to remember:

    —The "O.K." sign, with thumb and forefinger forming a circle is a rude gesture, especially when the other three fingers protrude outward, away from the body. This refers to a part of the female anatomy and is therefore considered a vulgar gesture.

—If a Brazilian man wishes to signal that he sees a pretty girl, he will cup both hands together to form a tube, or an imaginary telescope, and look through it at the girl with his eye.

—To add emphasis to a statement, a Brazilian may snap the fingers while whipping the hand down and out.

—If you see a Brazilian brush the back of his fingers under his chin and outward, he is indicating "I don't know."

—To express appreciation, a Brazilian may appear to pinch his earlobe between thumb and forefinger. For example, if you've enjoyed a meal this gesture may be used. Among Brazilians, to dramatize it even further, they will reach behind the head and grasp the opposite earlobe.

—Whipping the hand and fingers downward with the thumb and forefinger hitting each other is a way of signaling "That is a lot (or a great many, or a great deal)."

• The "fig," or *figa* as it is called in Brazil, with the hand forming a fist and with the thumb protruding upward between forefinger and middle finger is a symbol of *good luck* in Brazil. This is especially important to note because in some Mediterranean countries and even in certain other Latin countries, this is a rude, obscene gesture, regarded as a phallic symbol. But in Brazil, it is possible to buy replicas of this gesture in the form of charms or amulets because of its "good luck" symbolism.

• Punching the fist into a cupped hand is a vulgar gesture.

• When dining, avoid using the fingers to pick up any food unless you wrap it in a napkin. This is done for sanitary reasons and includes sandwiches and fruit.

- Never cut food with the side of your fork—always use a knife.

- When using toothpicks, always cover your mouth with a hand or napkin.

- Don't smoke during a meal. Brazilians customarily wait until the meal is finished.

- Again, for sanitary reasons, don't drink directly from a can or bottle. Even at roadside stops, glasses are usually furnished.

- If and when a toast is offered, it is sufficient to simply lift your glass, say *"salud,"* and sip the wine.

- Driving a car in Brazil is a rare—and very risky—experience. Rules of the road respected in many other countries are often good-naturedly disregarded in Brazil.

- When carrying any article along the streets—a pair of shoes, a bottle, a box of candy—it is customary to have it wrapped in a bag or some paper.

- As indicated, you will find Brazil a montage of gestures, so be aware and be certain to ask for interpretations if you spot some unknown signal.

Chile

- At the first introduction, a handshake is the customary greeting. Among close friends, an *abrazo* may also occur, along with a possible pat on the back. Men and women who are good friends, and two women will kiss one cheek, usually the right one.

- Men should note that when a woman enters the room, the polite gesture is to rise and be prepared to shake her hand *if* she offers it. A seated woman, however, need not rise nor is she obliged to offer her hand when a man enters.

- The customary Latin inclination toward "closeness" applies here, with people standing closer than Americans or Europeans do.

- Maintain good eye contact.

- Good posture while seated is also important.

- Yawns should be stifled or covered with the hand.

- Waiters may be beckoned with hand gestures, but others are beckoned more discreetly.

- Some important gestures in Chile are:

  —Making a fist and slapping it up into the palm of the other hand is a very rude gesture.

  —Holding the palm upward and then spreading the fingers signals that someone is "stupid."

  —If a Chilean driver holds his hand out the window as if he is holding a round object, he is making an obscene gesture.

  —Holding the fist upright level with the head is a Communist sign.

- When dining, one seldom eats anything with the fingers.

- If you pour wine, never do so with your left hand.

- Chilean wines are prized; if and when toasts are made, it is sufficient to simply raise your glass, look briefly at your host and others present, and say *"salud."*

Colombia

- A warm and friendly handshake is the custom in Colombia and is done frequently, especially on arriving and departing. Among male friends it will probably be a warm, friendly and lingering handshake, often accompanied by lightly grasping the other's forearm or elbow. Among close male friends, the handshake may be preceded (or followed) with an *abrazo,* or hug plus a couple of hearty claps on the shoulder or back.

- Colombian women will often substitute the gesture of holding forearms for a handshake.

- If you are visiting on business and happen to tour a factory, it is polite to shake hands with those workers nearest you.

- Etiquette and propriety are important in Colombia, therefore avoid placing your feet on a table or other piece of furniture, and avoid yawning in public and eating on the streets.

- To beckon someone, extend the arm, palm down, and move the fingers in a scratching motion.

- Some gestures that may be unique to Colombia are:

  —When using the hand to demonstrate how tall things are, the flat palm is held downward to show the height of *animals* but

205

never people. To show the height of a person the flat palm is held *sideways* (thumb on top).

—To show the *length* of something, most visitors would put two hands out, pointing the two index fingers, and letting the distance between the two fingers represent the distance. *This is considered a rude gesture in Colombia.* In Colombia, to show the length of something hold the right arm out, palm flat with thumb on top, and use the other hand to mark off the length along the right hand, wrist or forearm.

—Tapping the underside of the elbow with the fingers of the other hand suggests that someone is "stingy."

—If a Colombian holds a hand out, palm flat and pointing downward, and then takes his other hand and makes a sawing motion across the back of the first hand, it is a way of saying "Let's share or split the profits."

—Making the "O.K." signal with the thumb and forefinger making a circle, other fingers spread, and then placing the circle over your nose is a signal that someone else is a homosexual.

• When dining, many Colombians use the continental style of eating, with the fork always remaining in the left hand.

• Toasting is a simple matter of raising the glass, looking around at those closest to you, and saying "*salud,*" which means "health."

• To indicate that you have finished eating, place the knife and fork horizontally across the plate.

• Women visitors should be especially sensitive about making any glance or gesture that might be considered flirtatious.

Costa Rica

• Men shake hands. Costa Rican women pat left arms. Women who are good friends will kiss cheeks. Rural people will offer a slight bow and touch their hats.

- In business situations, formality rules. Don't expect *abrazos* here, and business jackets are usually kept on during business discussions.

- Exchange business cards, with yours printed in both English and Spanish.

- Don't ever put your feet up on any article of furniture.

- People usually queue in orderly lines for public transportation.

- Most American gestures—including rude ones—are known by Costa Ricans (who call themselves *"ticos"*). However, one gesture generally not used in the United States is the "fig" gesture where the hand is made into a fist and the thumb is forced upward to protrude between the forefinger and middle finger. This is a very rude gesture.

- When dining, conversation is common but it is impolite to talk with food in the mouth.

- Nude or partially nude sunbathing or swimming is regarded as extremely rude and improper.

- Local people bathe frequently each day because of the heat, and guests are expected to bathe at least once daily.

Ecuador

- As in other Latin countries, the handshake is the custom upon both arrivals and departures. Good male friends will embrace (the *abrazo*) and good female friends will embrace and kiss lightly on the cheek.

- Also, as in many Latin countries, touching and closeness are common. When conversing with an Ecuadorian, don't be surprised if he or she stands what you regard to be as unusually close. Casual touching of arms and shoulders is usually just a sign of friendship.

- Fidgeting with the hands is considered distracting, almost impolite. Same with the feet.

- When beckoning a waiter, you may observe that some patrons will clap their hands over their heads, but that is generally considered rude.

El Salvador

- The handshake is the common form of greeting here. North Americans and Europeans, accustomed to rather brief handshakes, may notice that Salvadorans, like many Latins, linger over the handshake. There may also be casual touching of the forearm and elbow as an acquaintanceship grows. Males who are good friends will probably embrace, the *abrazo*.

- Males are expected to rise from a seated position whenever a woman enters the room.

- Good eye contact is important in both social and business situations.

- Salvadorans are expressive with both hands and face, so watch for those signals that complement verbal communication.

- Yawning in social or business situations should be avoided.

- It is considered impolite to point the fingers—or the feet—at an object or a person.

- Many other gestures commonly used and known throughout Latin America will be known in El Salvador, so be familiar with those and then be watchful to see if they are rigidly practiced or simply known but not in daily use.

Guatemala

- A "hearty handshake" is the description often given to greetings in Guatemala. But this does not necessarily mean a strong, firm grip. Latins tend toward a more gentle grip than practiced by North Americans and some Europeans. Close male friends will also greet with an *abrazo*, accompanied by patting the back. Close female friends will hug lightly and brush cheeks as if kissing.

- Greetings here should also be accompanied by good eye contact, a friendly smile and genuine interest in the other person.

- It is best to ask permission before taking photographs of people. In fact, some people in the countryside will request a small payment in return.

- A soft voice is preferred to any loud, boisterous talking.

- To beckon someone, extend the arm, palm down and move the fingers in a scratching motion.

- When waving goodbye, the proper gesture is to raise your hand *with the palm facing you,* and then wave your fingers together back and forth.

- One gesture that should be avoided is the "fig" gesture. This is done by making a fist and then pushing the thumb up to protrude between the index and middle fingers. In some Mediterranean countries, this is considered a phallic symbol and is therefore terribly rude—as it is in Guatemala. However, in Brazil it is considered a sign meaning "Good luck."

- When being entertained, the female guest of honor will be seated to the right of the host and the male guest of honor to the host's left side.

- When dining, it is polite to finish everything on your plate.

- To attract a waiter, just raise your hand. In some less formal restaurants, patrons will make a sound like "cht, cht," but that is considered slightly impolite.

- Most North American gestures are understood in Guatemala.

Honduras

- As in most Latin countries, a warm but gentle handshake is the customary greeting. Close male friends will also embrace (the *abrazo*), while close female friends will hug lightly and offer a "pretend kiss" to the cheek.

- Personal space is smaller, and therefore North Americans and Northern Europeans may find Hondurans standing closer to them when conversing. This is merely a common trait and has no other significance.

- The "fig" gesture (hand making a fist with the thumb protruding between index and middle fingers) is an obscene and therefore insulting gesture.

- You may notice a Honduran waving an index finger back and forth in front of him, perhaps about chin level. This is a gesture signifying "no."

- If a Honduran takes one index finger, places it near the corner of his eye and seems to tug downward gently, this is a signal that is saying "Be careful. Watch out." Some males also may do this at women to be flirtatious.

- Bargaining is expected when shopping.
- Most Hondurans will be aware of common North American gestures.

Mexico

- A warm, somewhat soft handshake is the customary greeting among both men and women. Men should let the woman make the first move toward handshaking. After the second or third meeting, Mexican men may begin with or add the *abrazo,* the embrace along with a few pats on the back. Women friends will embrace lightly and pretend to kiss a cheek.
- In some areas of Mexico, you may encounter an unusual addition to the handshake where, after gripping the palm, the two people slide their hands upward to grasp each other's thumbs.
- Many Mexicans are "touch oriented." This means they may linger over a handshake, they may touch the forearm or elbow, or they may even casually finger the lapel of the other person's suit. All these touches merely signify a willingness to be friendly, nothing more.

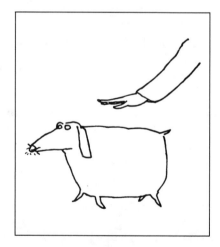

- When gesturing to indicate the height of an animal, Mexicans will extend the arm out, *palm downward,* at the designated height. This should *not* be used for the height of people, however. Instead, Mexicans will use a raised index finger.
- To beckon others, extend the arm, palm down, with the fingers making a scratching motion inward.
- In restaurants, there are two common methods for getting the attention of a waiter. The first is to make a "pssst-pssst" sound; the second is to make a kissing sound with the pursed lips. However, both of these, though common, are considered slightly impolite.

- While eating, both hands should be kept above the table, not in the lap.

- Mexicans are usually considered more open, more expressive than North Americans.

- When passing an object to another person, hand it to him or her—don't toss it. The same is true when handing over change—don't put it on the counter, place it in the hand.

- In public, men should not stand with their hands in their pockets.

- If a man stands with his hands on his hips, it suggests hostility or a challenge.

- Deference is shown to the elderly, so give way to them in public places and don't object if they are waited on first.

- Ask permission before photographing local people.

- Bargaining in stores is natural and expected.

- Never visit churches or religious sites while wearing short shorts, tank tops, or cut-off shirts or shorts.

- The national drink in Mexico is *tequila*. To drink it properly, here is the procedure: place a pinch of salt in the depression of your left hand between thumb and forefinger; then lick the salt and quickly take a drink of *tequila;* follow this by sucking on a lime wedge.

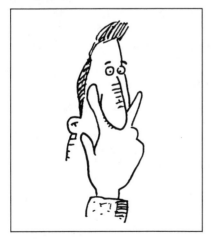

- A distinctive and very rude gesture in Mexico is as follows: make a "V" with the index and middle fingers with your palm facing you; then place the "V" over your nose.

- Patience is important; avoid showing anger if and when you encounter delays or interruptions.

- Nude bathing is very offensive to Mexicans.

- Many gestures common in North America have been imported across the border into Mexico, so they will be understood and, in many cases, even used.

Nicaragua

- The typical warm, friendly Latin handshake prevails here. Men who are close friends will embrace (the *abrazo*), and women friends will engage in a brief hug and cheek-kissing motion.

- Smiles are important when meeting others, and North Americans and Europeans may find that Nicaraguans stand closer together during gatherings and conversations. This merely reflects the Latin attitude toward personal space.

- Deference and respect is shown to the elderly with many actions and gestures: rising when they enter the room, opening doors, and giving up seats on public transportation.

- As in other Central American countries, one obscene gesture is the "fig." This is the label given to the fist when the thumb protrudes upward between the index and middle fingers. It is a phallic symbol, and therefore considered an offensive and rude gesture.

- Eye contact is important at all times.

- Most American gestures are known here, with many of them in common daily use.

Panama

- A nod, a handshake, and the *abrazo* are all used in Panama for daily greetings. A nod and mildly firm handshake is the most common, while the *abrazo,* or embrace is frequently exchanged among good male friends. Women friends will embrace lightly, and make a kissing-like motion to one cheek.

- Women should avoid wearing clothing that is revealing.

- When dining the host usually sits at one end of the table with the guest of honor at the other end.

- Because of the long North American presence in Panama, most American gestures will be known and understood.

Paraguay

- Handshaking is not only the common greeting but done, as in many Latin countries, on both arriving and departing. Men shake hands with other men and also with women. Women friends will embrace briefly and brush cheeks in a "pretend kiss."

- Paraguayans will usually stand very close to you during conversations.

- Two gestures that may cause *offense* are as follows:

  —Crossing the middle finger over the index finger as North Americans and certain Europeans do to say or signal "Good luck."

  —The "O.K." gesture, with thumb and forefinger forming a circle is considered rude.

- If you cross your legs while seated, cross them knee-over-knee instead of propping one ankle on top of the other knee.

- Try to keep your feet on the floor, and never prop them on a piece of furniture.

- Good, erect posture is important while seated, and don't sit on desks, tables or other articles of furniture.

- Tilting the head backward signifies "I forgot."

- Winking is usually only done for romantic or sexual connotations.

- If a Paraguayan brushes his fingers under his chin and then outward, he is saying "I don't know."

- When dining, the continental style (fork constantly in the left hand) is customary here.

- Don't keep your hands in your lap while eating. Rest the wrists lightly on the table—but never the elbows.

- Exhibit patience in all your actions.

Peru

- Both men and women shake hands when greeting and when departing. Men who are good friends will add or even substitute an *abrazo* or hug accompanied by some hearty patting on the back. Women will hug lightly and brush cheeks as if kissing.

Children will often kiss elders as a greeting, even if they have not met before. North Americans and Europeans may unintentionally perform what has been called the "conversational tango" with people in Peru. That is because Peruvians, and many other Latins, tend to stand very close together when conversing. This makes Americans and Europeans very uncomfortable, so they back off. The Latin follows, and the visitor retreats again. As a visitor, try to avoid this lest you silently signal to your "partner" that you don't like him or his conversation.

- Men and women in Peru may be seen walking arm-in-arm with people of the same sex. This merely expresses friendship.

- When walking alongside a woman, "well-bred" men will walk with a protective hand under her elbow, which she should obligingly bend.

- In either social or business conversation, good eye contact is important.

- When seated, crossing the legs is acceptable but it is customary to cross them at the knees—not with one ankle propped on the other knee.

- If you want to beckon someone, extend the arm, palm down, and wiggle the fingers in a scratching motion.

- If you smoke cigarettes, offer them to those around you before smoking. The same with candy.

- If and when photographing members of the Indian population, be certain to obtain permission first. The village mountain people believe photographing children will take their souls away.

- Tapping the index finger to the temple means he or she is crazy. But, tapping the index finger to the middle of the forehead means he or she is "dumb" or "stupid."

- Shaking the hand up and down at the wrist with the fingers flapping, if done slowly, means "What a lot!" But if done rapidly and with the elbow raised, it means "Oh, boy, we're in for it."

- Gestures noted in other Latin countries that are also used in Peru are:

  —Tapping the underside of the elbow with the fingers means "cheap" or "stingy."

  —Tugging the corner of the eye downward with a finger means "Be careful," or "Look out."

  —Pointing can be done by pursing the lips and motioning in the desired direction.

- When dining, keep your hands above the table. The best position is with wrists lightly on the table. No elbows on the table.

- To signal that you have finished eating, place your knife and fork in parallel across your plate.

Puerto Rico

- The handshake is the customary greeting here. Old friends may embrace, the *abrazo*. Women friends may embrace lightly and brush cheeks, as if kissing.

- As in most Latin countries, people tend to stand close to one another in any social or even business setting. This relates to a different perspective on "personal space," with North Americans and many Europeans believing that people should stand about an arm's length from one another. If you tend to move away from a Latin, it could be considered as offensive or insulting.

- Some unique gestures to know in Puerto Rico are as follows:

  —Men tend to smile and stare at women, which is considered acceptable, but the reverse is not.

  —Puerto Ricans tend to interrupt each other frequently and are not upset when this occurs.

  —When handing small items to people, never toss or throw them.

  —To beckon someone, the fingers are waved downward.

  —If someone wiggles their nose, it probably means he or she is saying "What's going on here?"

  —To point, instead of using the hand and index finger, a Puerto Rican may purse the lips and motion toward the object with the mouth.

—You will hear restaurant patrons signal for waiters by making a "psssst" sound.

- Because of the close economic and political ties with the United States, most American gestures will be known and possibly used in parts of Puerto Rico.

Uruguay

- A warm and friendly handshake is the custom in Uruguay among both men and women. Good male friends will hug; women will do the same, adding a "pretend" kiss on the cheeks.

- When young people are introduced in Uruguay, girls may kiss one another, and boys may give brotherly kisses to the girls. Young men, however, will shake hands.

- Physical closeness is also common here, so people will stand close together in both social and business situations.

- To signal to a waiter, simply raise your hand. Some locals may make a kissing sound, but it is considered rude.

- Many North American gestures, as described in Chapter 2, will be recognized here. For example, the "thumb's up" signal is well-known and used in Uruguay. Similarly, because of its close proximity to Brazil, Uruguayans will consider the "O.K." symbol a very rude gesture.

Venezuela

- People greet one another here with a warm, somewhat gentle but friendly handshake. Men who know each other well may pat the right shoulder of the other person as well. Good male friends will embrace, the *abrazo*. Men and women who are good friends may kiss, and good women friends will hug lightly and kiss cheeks. Be sure to shake hands when arriving and when departing as well.

- Maintaining good eye contact during business or social discussions is considered both polite and important.

- As in many Latin countries, posture while seated is important. Try to keep the feet well planted on the floor, and avoid slouching or placing your foot on a chair or desk.

- When dining, wait for everyone else at the table to be served before beginning to eat.

- To indicate you have finished eating, place your utensils in parallel and diagonally across your plate.

- It is better to conduct business in person rather than over the telephone.

- Closeness and casual touching among males will be seen in Venezuela just as in most Latin countries. Men should be very careful about public physical contact with women, however.

THE UNITED STATES AND CANADA

Canada (Western and Atlantic Provinces)

- A firm handshake plus direct eye contact is the standard form of greeting in Canada. Men should shake hands with women if they offer their hand, but many women will just say "hello," perhaps with a nod of the head, and not shake hands.

- Distances are farther apart than in Latin America or the Far East. When conversing, people will stand about a half meter apart.

- There is little or no casual touching. The only exceptions are that good male friends may occasionally pat the other's back, close relatives may put their arms around another's shoulder, and good female friends may occasionally hug when greeting each other after long intervals.

- Good eye contact is important, whether it is during business or social conversation.

- In social situations, men will usually rise when women enter a room.

- Canadians in these provinces are described as "friendly," "somewhat reserved," and "on the conservative side." Therefore, excessive gesturing is not common.

- Men will sit with legs crossed, and all three forms are common and accepted: crossed at the ankles, crossed at the knees, and having one ankle crossed on the other knee.

- Beckoning is done by raising the hand, *fingers pointing up and palm inward,* and motioning the fingers toward one's face or body. This contrasts with the beckoning signal in many other parts of the world where the arm is extended, palm down, and the fingers are moved in a scratching motion.

- To beckon a waiter, just raise the hand at or above head level. To signal that you want the check, make a motion with the hands as if you are signing a piece of paper.

- Canadians may eat with either the continental style (fork constantly in the left hand) or the American style (where the fork moves back and forth between the hands).

- Most of the popular gestures shown in Chapter 2 will be known, used and fully understood in Canada. The one exception might be the "hook 'em horns" gesture known in the United States (especially in Texas), and in Italy, Africa, and Brazil.

Canada (Quebec)

- Since the French culture is so strong in this province, certain actions associated with Europe may be noted here. A firm handshake is still the common and preferred method of greeting, but it may be done more often (e.g., at both arrivals and departures, and in all social situations). Also, close male friends may embrace lightly when meeting, and women may do the same, while adding a light kissing motion to the cheek.

- French-speaking Canadians may seem more reserved than their American neighbors to the south, with more emphasis on all aspects of etiquette.

- It is considered bad manners to eat while on the street.

- To beckon a waiter, nod the head backward slightly, or raise your hand discreetly.

- When dining, the continental style of eating will probably prevail, although some Canadians will shift the fork back and forth American-style.

- Most of the more common gestures pictured in Chapter 2 will be known, understood and even used by Canadians.

United States

- A firm handshake, accompanied by direct eye contact, is the standard greeting in the United States. Occasionally, among very good friends who have not seen each other for long intervals, women may briefly hug other women, and men may quickly kiss the cheek of a woman. Males rarely hug one another, however. Occasionally, men may shake hands with the left hand either covering the handshake or lightly gripping the forearm.

This represents a higher degree of warmth and friendship, and politicians may be seen using this technique when campaigning.

- According to anthropologists, Americans tend to stand just about one arm's length away from each other while conversing or standing in public. It's called "the comfort zone."

- In the past decade, much emphasis has been placed on sexual equality in the workplace. While many women still enjoy having men open doors for them, help them get seated, and give up seats in public transportation, there are some women who object to such deference.

- Speaking of exceptions, because the United States has such ethnic diversity, visitors may also occasionally observe people greeting each other with hugs and cheek-kissing. Certain nationalities have brought these customs to the United States and continue to practice them, but they are not in wide use.

- Probably the only circumstance where two men may be seen walking in public and holding hands is if they are openly homosexual.

- Direct eye contact in both social and business situations is very important. Not doing so implies boredom or disinterest.

- Americans generally respect queues or lines in public situations and will form lines in an orderly fashion. To shove or push one's way into such a line will probably generate both anger and verbal complaints.

- There are two well-known rude and insulting gestures in the United States. Both are recognized in all parts of America. They are:

—The middle finger thrust.

—The forearm jerk.

- Waving "hello" or "good-bye" is done by extending the arm, palm facing down, and waving the hand up and down at the wrist joint. Another variation is to raise the arm, palm outward, and move the whole arm and hand back and forth like an upside down pendulum. This may be important to

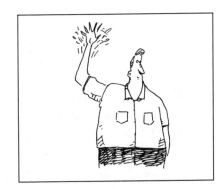

know because in many other countries this is a signal for "no."

- Many Americans become uncomfortable with periods of silence. Therefore in business or social situations, if a gap occurs they will quickly try to fill in with conversation.

- Winking in America can signal diverse messages: flirtation, friendliness, amusement, or to signal "I am just kidding."

- When driving, automobiles are equipped with flashing lights as turning signals. If these are not operating, or if cyclists wish to signal for a turn, the proper procedure is as follows: extending the left arm straight out of the driver's window means "I plan to turn to the left," but if the arm is bent *upward* it signals "I plan to turn to the right."

- Beckoning can be done by either raising the index finger and repeatedly curling it in and out, or by raising the hand (palm facing inward) and waggling the fingers back toward the body. Either is acceptable.

- To call a waiter, just raise one hand to head level or above. To signal that you want the check, make a writing motion with two hands (one hand representing the paper, the other making a writing motion).

- When dining, many Americans are taught to keep the left hand in their lap and eat with the right hand. It is permissible to sit at a table with both wrists resting lightly on the table. When engaged in deep, close conversation, two people might even lean forward, with elbows on the table, but strict practitioners of etiquette in America frown on this.

- It is considered impolite to use toothpicks in front of other people.

- It has become an important courtesy in the United States to ask permission of your host or hostess before smoking.

- Using the hand and index finger to point at objects or to point directions is perfectly common and acceptable.

- Two popular sports in the United States are baseball and football. Both have a special set of unique signals used by the officials—called umpires and referees, respectively—to indicate to onlookers what is happening on the playing field. A spectator can usually find the explanation for each of these signals in the printed program sold at such sporting events.

- To signal across a distance that "You have a telephone call," Americans will usually point at the person and then hold the other hand up to the jaw and mouth as if holding a telephone receiver.

- Whistling is common, either as a method for hailing the attention of someone at a distance, as an accompaniment to applause or cheering, or as a form of personal entertainment. Whistling is *not* intended as a form of vocal derision as it is, say, in Europe. In the United States, crowds voice disapproval by shouting out the word "booooo!"

- If an American is seen holding both hands to the throat, this is the signal for "I am choking." It might be seen, for instance, in sporting events as a sarcastic signal that someone is showing tension and playing poorly. But it can be used in a far more serious situation. Health experts in the United States are urging people to use—and to recognize—this gesture if and when a person is choking on a piece of food. In such a situation, the person cannot talk and is signaling "Help!"

- Mothers will scold children by shaking an index finger at them. People will admire children by patting them on the top of the head.

- One commonly used hand gesture for signaling "no" is to wave the forearm and hand (palm outward) in front and across the upper body, back and forth.

- Other popular gestures illustrated in Chapter 2, such as the "O.K." sign, "V for victory" and "thumbs up," are all very popular and well-known throughout the United States. The "hook 'em horns" gesture is associated with the state of Texas. The "hang loose" gesture is known and used in the state of Hawaii but not generally known in the other 49 states of the United States.

Additional Reading

Asian Customs & Manners, Kevin Chambers (Meadowbrook, 1988) is an excellent guidebook.

European Customs & Manners, Nancy D. Braganti and Elizabeth Devine (Meadowbrook, 1984) is a fine guidebook.

HarperCollins Business Guide To Moscow (Harper & Row, 1990). An indispensable guide to anyone traveling to that capital city.

Latin American Customs & Manners, Elizabeth Devine and Nancy L. Braganti (St. Martin's Press, 1988) is another excellent area-specific guidebook.

Times Books International, in Singapore and Kuala Lumpur, has produced an excellent series of books for several Far Eastern countries, including Thailand, Singapore, Malaysia, Korea, and Japan. Each is titled *Culture Shock*, and each is written by different authors. Each book is jammed with information on all aspects of culture and behavior for that country.

Looking at Each Other, Marion E. Current and Choi Dong-ho, published by the Seoul International Tourist Publishing Co., is a valuable handbook for anyone visiting South Korea or dealing with Koreans.

Understanding Arabs, A Guide for Westerners, Margaret K. Nydell (Intercultural Press Inc., Yarmouth, ME, 1987) provides just what the title proposes.

The Economist (Magazine) Business Traveller's Guides, published by Prentice Hall Press are excellent handbooks when traveling or doing business internationally. Separate books have been published for the following areas: Britain, France, Germany, China, Japan, Southeast Asia, the United States, and the Arabian Peninsula.

Index